D1084186

NOAH WEBSTER

FATHER OF THE DICTIONARY

A typical American farm boy who made good under difficulties, Noah Webster's influence in the development of the United States was a real contribution to its growth. His life covers a fascinating period in American history when the young republic was just getting on its feet. Where others gave the new country its laws and government, he provided schoolbooks glowing with the American spirit. Twenty-five million copies of Webster's *Spelling Book* were used in schools during his lifetime. The *American Dictionary,* which he compiled when he was fifty years of age, was his greatest achievement.

NOAH WEBSTER

Father of the Dictionary

BY

ISABEL PROUDFIT

Illustrated by

I. B. Hazelton

PILGRIM INSTITUTE
52549 Gumwood Road
Granger, Indiana 46530

PUBLISHED BY PILGRIM INSTITUTE
52549 GUMWOOD ROAD, GRANGER, INDIANA 46530

BY PERMISSION OF
JULIAN MESSNER, INC., NEW YORK

PRINTED IN THE UNITED STATES OF AMERICA

Contents

CHAPTER ONE

A Boy with a Hoe

IN A FIELD below a red farmhouse, one July morning long ago, a boy of twelve was hoeing corn. Up one row and down another in the steaming heat of a summer day, he broke the ground around each stalk, destroying the weeds that might have choked it.

Overhead the sun beat down out of a cloudless sky. The birds in the orchard, who sang so cheerfully in the early morning, were silent. Yet the boy, whose name was Noah Webster, did not complain. He knew that this was good "growing weather." Plenty of sun in July brought a rich harvest in September, and without that rich harvest the farmers round about, his own family in the red farmhouse, might suffer during the winter.

[3]

Sun and rain, heat and cold, had little meaning for him, excepting as they affected the crops. For himself he could perspire freely and drink great draughts of water from the jug in the fence corner, if it were warm; grease his boots and wrap a muffler around his head, if it were wet. But the young corn was different. Planted delicately in the warm earth of spring, it demanded the most careful tending.

All farming was like that, he thought, as he stopped to mop his hot forehead. The tobacco in the next field, which his father grew for export to England, required even more careful tending than the corn. There were animals, too, which must be cared for—horses and sheep and cows and oxen. The long daylight hours were never long enough to get the work done. Even though there were two brothers besides himself to help their father, the farm took all their strength and energy.

This was a great pity, thought Noah, because there were so many other things in the world as important as farming. Books and reading, for example. Although he had probably never seen more than a dozen books in his life, Noah Webster liked reading. He could think for hours about words and their meaning. A printed page was to him exciting new country. But how could he explore this new country when there were always animals to feed, corn to hoe, tools to mend or sharpen every waking moment? Only when darkness shut down at last could he hope to spend a few moments by the candle in the kitchen, or in his bedroom, reading whatever he could lay his hands on.

His brothers, Abram and Charles, did not agree with him about this. When he read in the bedroom at night, they only grunted and asked him to blow out the candle. But their small, wiry middle brother was not easily diverted. Shading the light with his hand, he plowed earnestly down whatever page he happened to be reading.

Fortunately for the brothers, there was often nothing at all for him to read in this manner. In the Connecticut Colony in the year 1771, books were rare and precious articles. Every family, of course, had a Bible on a special shelf in the parlor. The minister, too, had books, perhaps twenty of them, mostly written in Latin. In the school-house by the church there were three books: a primer, from which the small children learned their letters, a speller and a Psalter for the older children.

Yet every week there came a newspaper from Hartford, and every Christmas brought a fresh copy of *Ames Almanack* to hang on a nail behind the kitchen door. This calendar contained notes about the weather for the coming year and a number of miscellaneous items sand-wiched in around the days of the month. Maxims such as his mother quoted freely, poetry about the stars or heaven, an article on fertilizer or paper-making perhaps, a description of a dwarf born and living in Massachusetts.

Long before July of any year, however, Noah had read the *Almanack* through many times. Even when he was

a little boy too young to read, he had watched his mother
turn a page each month, and asked eagerly:

"What does it *say*, Ma? What does it say *now?*"

"Mercy, child, nothing a shaver like you would want
to hear."

"Oh, but I *do* want to hear it. Read it to me! Read it!"

"Well, now, let me see. My spectacles are in the parlor,
and doubtless the bread is burning. . . . Here, here is
something. 'Cash will be paid for rags, coarse or fine, old
Sail Cloth, Cotton or Checks, to use in making paper by
the new mill at Milton. . . .' Well, we haven't any rags
to spare."

"What else does it say, Ma?"

"Here is an article on perspiration. Perspiration, it
says, is different from sweat. Sweat is weakening. . . .
Now, who would have thought that!"

"What else does it say, Ma?"

"Here is a piece on farming. 'The Glory of the World
Will be transplanted to America.' What has that to do
with farming?" Mrs. Webster bent closer to the page.
"Oh, it goes on to say 'The Study and Practice of Agri-
culture must go hand in hand with our increase' . . .
Sakes alive, child. I *told* you the bread would burn."

And snatching up the long bread-shovel from the
hearth, she opened the door of the Dutch oven in the
chimney. . . .

That was in 1764, when Noah was six years old. Now
that he was twelve, he read the *Almanack* for himself as

soon as it came each December. This year's *Almanack* had been full of good maxims:

> God helps them that help themselves.
>
> The Sleeping Fox catches no Poultry.
>
> Handle your Tools without Mittens—the
> Cat in gloves catches no mice.

There was also an essay urging more colleges for the study of medicine.

Noah already knew about the colleges that existed in the Colonies—Princeton College in New Jersey, Columbia in New York City, Harvard in Cambridge, Massachusetts, and Yale in his own Colony of Connecticut. The ministers, who preached in the parish church, were always college men, quoting Greek and Latin from the pulpit over the heads of the innocent farmers. Noah did not care so much for these quotations, but he liked the Bible stories the minister read before the long sermon. Abraham talking with God on the mountain. Noah guiding the animals into the ark before the great flood. Try as he might he could not think of himself as like that gray-bearded man in the Old Testament. Why had his mother and father chosen the name Noah for him? It was his father's name, too, of course, but still he did not like it.

Better than anything in the Old Testament were the

splendid Psalms, which the minister intoned with such feeling.

I have lifted up mine eyes unto the hills.

Noah felt like that when he looked out across his father's fields to Talcott Mountain across the valley. It was not that he did not love his native home, the rich valley of the Connecticut River with the town of Hartford east of them, and his own village of West Hartford here around him. It was only that words to describe his feelings were crowded out by the endless work of the farm. That work was waiting for him now; he had been a long time dreaming.

Sighing a little, he plunged his hoe into the soft earth, for he was not a lazy boy. "Stick-to-it-iveness," his mother always said, was one of his major qualities. It was a quality she admired in her son, for she wanted him to be strong and manly. Mrs. Webster was a practical, hard-working woman, who believed in facing life squarely. The year's maxim, *God helps them that help themselves,* was one to which she gave hearty approval.

A rabbit, starting up out of a hole at his feet, interrupted Noah a moment later. In a flash he was after her. He could not catch her, of course, merely follow her zig-zag course through the young corn a short way and then come back to his hoeing. Before starting again, however, he stooped to examine the hole from which she sprang. There were four baby rabbits huddled together there in a snug nest of dry grass. Carefully replacing the earth around them, he went on down the row, humming a little under his breath as he worked.

The song he hummed had a nice lilt to it, although the words were not very sensible. They were about a man who had drunk too much rum and molasses in the town taverns. The tune went like this:

There was a man in o ur town, I pi · ty his con · di · tion

People called this song the *Yankee Song,* and anyone who played a flute, as his brother Abram did, liked to play it in the evening after supper.

CHAPTER TWO

No Broth, No Ball

THE DINNER BELL sounding from the house on the ridge above him brought Noah quickly up the slope through the orchard at noontime. The fields of the Webster farm—ninety rich acres—lay below this ridge. The ridge formed the main street of the village, a brown country road with houses on either side of it.

Behind every house there was an orchard. How often Noah had played out under the apple trees with his brothers and sisters in the summer. But now that he was twelve, he must work in the fields when he was not in school. The short summers and long winters of New England made farming a serious business.

Pausing outside the kitchen door to wash his hands in a tin basin, the boy went in through the hot kitchen to the dining-room beyond it. This dining-room was really the winter kitchen of the house, but it made a cool room in which to eat during the summer. Here his father and brothers were gathering noisily at the table, while his older sister, Mercy, brought in the soup.

Noah looked with some distaste at the steaming bowls which held broth with a cornmeal dumpling floating in it. After the broth there would be boiled meat and vegetables, with perhaps a thick pudding, called hasty pudding, for dessert. In a New England household of that day there was no catering to delicate appetites. The soup was made from the water in which the meat and vegetables were boiled. One iron pot took care of all the cooking. If the midday dinner today was like the dinner yesterday and tomorrow no-one complained. Yet to Noah this was something of a hardship; he had always been what his mother called a "finicky" eater.

"Come now, Noah, eat up," she said, noticing that he was tasting his soup half-heartedly. "You know the saying: 'No broth, no ball; no ball, no meat.' "

By "ball" she meant the cornmeal dumpling in the soup, which some people considered a great delicacy. The "meat," of course, was the boiled beef and potatoes and cabbage, which would follow.

"You know I don't relish hot victuals on a hot day," answered Noah a little peevishly. "I'd rather just bread and a mug of cider."

"That's no meal after a morning's work," answered his mother. "Come now, show more sperit. There's a fresh copy of the *Connecticut Courant* on the dresser. You'll have that to read tonight, after your father has seen it."

"Let the boy read it, when he will," answered the father heavily. "There's too much politics in the paper nowadays. It roils a man to read it."

"Still the taxes on tea and molasses!" said the mother. "Will the government never learn that we won't be taxed unfairly!"

"But why is it unfair to tax us, Ma?" asked Noah.

"Because we have no deputies in the British Parliament. If we could send men there to represent us, we would feel easier about the whole matter."

"I tell you our charters as Colonies are being violated!" cried Mr. Webster.

"What does 'violated' mean, Pa?" asked Noah, his eyes sparkling with interest.

"It means breaking a promise."

"Did the British government promise never to tax us?"

"They promised us fair and open government. We no longer have that in the Colonies!"

"But is a little tax on tea so bad, Pa? People hereabouts mostwise drink cider."

"A little tax on tea is nothing. But likely soon there will be other taxes. Already there have been taxes on glass and sugar and paper. People did without them until the tax was lifted. But someday there will be taxes on things we can't do without—coal or iron or salt or silver. There is the question of the soldiers, too. Every day more soldiers come for us to house and victual."

"Soldiers!" cried Noah. "What do we want with soldiers?"

"We don't want them. Years ago they helped us fight the Indians. Now they come to collect taxes!"

"In Boston they call them 'lobsters,' on account of their red coats, said Mrs. Webster. "The sight of them miffs the people. . . . Dear me, look at your dish. A bird pecking at crumbs would eat more than you have."

"I'll eat more for supper, Ma, honest Injun," answered Noah, sliding out of his chair and reaching into the cupboard for a handful of raisins. "I'll be getting back to the corn now."

"See that you do then," answered his mother.

"Bread and milk taste good after the hoeing," said Noah. "With some of your good relish for sweetening."

His mother watched him affectionately, as he went out through the orchard. This middle son of hers was different from his four brothers and sisters. So quick and eager about so many things: he was a born "investigator."

She remembered well the October day when he was born. Lying in the big bed in the parlor, from which she could see easily into the kitchen, she watched the morning sun slant in through the windows. The baby in the cradle beside her seemed to watch the sun, too.

One by one during the afternoon of that day neighbors came in to congratulate her, and to drink a mug of cider with her husband. Indeed several of them had been there all day, caring for the new baby, taking her place in the kitchen. Whether or not there was a new baby in the family, the work of the farm must go on. The smell of bread baking in the oven, clothes drying before the fire, apples stewing for supper, reached her.

October was a good month in which to have a new baby. It would not be so cold tomorrow when he was carried to the church for baptism. The church was nearly four miles away. How she had suffered two years before, when little Jerusha was carried out into the cold in January to be baptized. The minister had had to break the ice in the bowl of water before he could perform the ceremony.

She had always wondered a little if it were really necessary to baptize a new baby quite so soon after he was born. Or if, indeed, it must be done on that day, might it not be done at home? But no-one had ever dared suggest that an infant be baptized other than in church and on the day after he was born.

One thing she was quite sure of. People could say what they liked, it was *not* good for young children to be dipped head first in a tub of cold water when they were ill! The feet might be dipped in—yes. After all, wet and cold feet never seemed to hurt anyone. But the old-fashioned dipping of the head in water upset a sick child terribly. Often the crying which followed seemed to make them worse, in spite of the treatment.

An October baby, however, who was reasonably healthy, did not require any such treatment. Why, then, did the *Almanack* for that year speak of October as "an unlucky Season"? She had never found it so. October brought the ripe harvests of field and orchard, the weather was cool and clear, the work not quite so strenuous. And this year a new little son, named for his father, had come to join the family.

Searching the *Almanack* further for some omen about the boy's birth, she did find something that pleased her. "A Thought upon the past, present, and future State of North America," it offered.

Arts and Sciences will change the Face of Nature from here to the Western Ocean; and as they march thru the vast Desert, the Residence of Wild Beasts will be broken up, and their obscene Howl cease for ever;—Instead of which the Stones and Trees will dance together at the Music of Orpheus, the Rocks will disclose their hidden gems, and the Treasures of Gold and Silver be broken up. Huge Mountains of Iron Ore are already discovered. This metal, more useful than Gold and Silver, will imploy millions of Hands, not only to form the martial Sword and peaceful Plow, alternately; but an infinity of Utensils, improved in the Exercise of Art, and Handicraft among Men . . . Shall not then those vast quarries, that teem with Stone—those for structure be piled into Great Cities—and those for Sculpture into Statues to perpetuate the Honor of renowned Heroes; even those who shall now save Their Country.

Yes, an important country had important men, as well as big cities and rich industries. Her baby, lying now in his cradle, might well become one of those men. She would watch and wait for him to grow into one. . . .

Meanwhile, there was the never-ending work of the house to keep her busy. Cooking and cleaning and washing were only a part of it. There were cloth and clothes to make, soap and lard and butter and candles, fruit to put up, corn and herbs to dry, wood fires to keep burning.

When Noah was born there were already two sisters, nine and two years old, and a brother Abram, seven years old, in the family. After Noah came another brother, Charles, four years younger than he was. By the time Noah was twelve, all the children did their full share of work. Mercy and Jerusha, the daughters, could do anything their mother did. Abram, at nineteen, was a tireless young farmer. Noah could plow and plant corn, rake hay, milk, help to butcher or shear sheep, and make syrup in springtime. Charles at eight drove the cows to pasture, weeded the garden, carried wood and water.

Mr. Webster, a tall, good-humored Yankee, full of salt wisdom, did what all the other farmers in West Hartford did each year. In the summer he bent his back to the crops. In the winter he made tools and harness, barrels and buckets of wood, shoes and even furniture.

Fun for the boys came chiefly in the fall, when they went hunting. In the winter they might skate a little on a nearby pond. The girls liked the husking-bees in the late summer, when jolly young farmers came to strip the corn and eat enormously of the good food the womenfolk provided. Election Day was nice, too; so were Christmas and Pope's Day on the fifth of November.

Hallowe'en was not yet celebrated. Neither was there any Fourth of July. When young Noah Webster stood hoeing his father's corn in July, 1771, it was still five years before the Declaration of Independence was written!

CHAPTER THREE

Patriotic Protests

AFTER SUPPER THAT July night, Noah carried the Hartford paper out into the front yard to read under the big Kentucky coffee-bean tree there. The Webster house was over a hundred years old; there were lovely trees growing around it. The Kentucky coffee-bean tree, however, was Noah's favorite, because of its rough bark and mysterious habit of coming to life in the spring. Long after the maple trees had unfurled their new leaves, it remained bare and forbidding. Then, suddenly, answering some mysterious summons, it burst into leaf at last.

Noah often thought that a New England spring was like that, too. There would be ice and snow for many months—often snow in April. Then suddenly spring was upon them. It took faith to believe that spring would come to the snow-bound fields at last. The kind of faith which his ancestors brought with them, when they came out from England to settle in this new country.

Noah's relatives were among the earliest settlers of Connecticut. His great-great-grandfather had been governor of the State in the year 1656.

Noah loved to hear tales of the early days, when Connecticut was founded by his great-great-grandfather and others. In 1635, so his father said, a party of brave men set out from Boston to found a settlement further south. Traveling on foot for many days, through forests and swamps and across rivers, they managed to cover a hundred miles to the Connecticut River valley, where they founded the town of Newe Towne, later called Hartford.

The journey was unlike any Noah had heard of. The men carried packs of clothing on their backs, as well as rifles and cooking utensils. In front of them they drove 160 head of cattle. Later on their other goods came around by water. In the meantime they had only the clothes they stood in, and a campfire at night to make them cheerful.

Hostile Indians still lived in the forests through which they traveled. It would be necessary to protect their new homes from them, too. And after the new homes were built there was the great task of clearing the land for farming. Each acre must be wrestled free of trees and brush and stones for planting. In the blood and bones of boys like Noah Webster was the knowledge that farmland did not come for the asking. Weeks of patient labor were necessary to clear a single field; every time the land was plowed a fresh crop of stones littered the ground. Men who farmed in New England knew that someone's back-breaking work had given them their fields.

The houses, too, which had been built on these farms, cost plenty of effort. A great central chimney usually formed the backbone of these houses. In front, on either side of the entrance, there was a parlor and a bedroom. Behind, a roomy kitchen ran the full length of the house. Upstairs—so cold and remote in wintertime—there were usually two bedrooms, one for the girls in the family, one for the boys. Sick people never slept upstairs in these cold bedrooms. If the bedroom downstairs was crowded, there might be a bed in the parlor or kitchen, where an ailing child or grandmother lay in comfort during an illness.

The kitchen was always the center of family-life in New England. Here a great open fire blazed perpetually in the fireplace. Over the fire swung a kettle of boiling water or a pot of food, cooking. Bread was baked in the Dutch oven beside the fireplace, or in the hot ashes beneath the fire itself. Hams and bacon hung in the chimney high above the fire for smoking.

Naturally, with so much going on in the kitchen, the furniture had to be simple. A bench for milk pans and water, a cupboard for food, a table at which to eat. Stools by the fireplace, with perhaps an armchair for the father of the family. A bed in the far corner, a cradle for the newest baby. Even in Noah's time, over a hundred years after Connecticut was settled, the family kitchen was much the same as it had been for generations.

The cooking was done in iron kitchen utensils, which had to be brought over from England. Every family had an iron kettle, an iron pot, and an iron frying pan, called

The kitchen was always the center of family life in New England.

a skillet. These might well last a lifetime. When Noah's sisters were married they would carry with them to their new homes three new iron utensils and a chest of quilts and bedding, made with their own hands. Buckets and tubs for their new homes, beds and chairs and tables, would be made by the young men they married.

Doubtless the young men would build the new homes, too, with the help of the neighbors. Fortunate it was, perhaps, that the houses of that period were all so much alike. A girl who married could count on having a roomy kitchen, a parlor and a bedroom on the ground floor of her house, with an open fireplace in each room to warm it. Upstairs under the eaves there would be the two modest bedrooms. Closets and bathrooms were unknown. Stoves were still not common when Noah was a boy. But home was home in spite of these drawbacks, and the red farmhouse on the ridge, which was home to him for many years, held a great deal of simple comfort.

Sitting out under the big tree, reading, Noah thought again of how Connecticut and the other American Colonies were founded. Sons and grandsons of his great-great-grandfather Webster were scattered all through New England—thickly around Hartford, farther away in Massachusetts.

The Colonies, the newspaper said, were no longer getting fair treatment from the mother country. This grave matter of taxation, for instance. If tea were taxed, why not salt and spices, silk for his mother's Sunday bonnet, books, too, and paper? People were collecting rags in Massachusetts for a new paper-mill there, but it might not succeed after all. Others were trying to grow silk-worms, but the climate was not suitable for the mulberry bushes on which the worms fed.

Now the soldiers were in Boston,, trying to put down the riots which occurred when the king's agents came to collect the taxes. Their red coats were everywhere. People resented their presence. When they walked down the street, water from scrubbing pails sometimes flew disastrously out of upstairs windows; pretty girls whom they would have liked to call on shut the doors in their faces.

A group of men in Boston had formed a secret society, called the Sons of Liberty. These men made it very plain what they thought of the king's agents. Three times in those hectic years before the Revolution, men who sympathized with the government were taken from their homes at night and tarred-and-feathered. Pulled roughly from a warm bed, they were carried far out of town and covered with a coat of warm tar. Then feathers from a plump pillow or two were poured over them. It took hours of painful work to clean the tar and feathers off afterward.

News of these doings were reported faithfully in the weekly papers all through the Colonies. Out under the coffee-bean tree that July night Noah Webster read eagerly the news of the Colonies.

CHAPTER FOUR

The One-Room School-House

I N OCTOBER, WHEN he was thirteen, Noah went back to the village school for what he thought would be his last year of "learning." Boys of fourteen in New England were almost men. No longer could they idle away precious hours at school.

The school was a one-room building beside the church, drafty in winter, blazing hot in summer when the younger children came at seven in the morning to learn their ABCs from a primer. The bigger boys came chiefly in winter, when they were not needed at home. Fall harvesting or spring plowing drew them away from the classroom.

Beside the school-house in the fall there was a wood-pile almost as big as the school itself. Every family with children in the school brought a load of wood every autumn. This wood for the fireplace, and a pail of water in the corner, furnished what comfort the school afforded. No wonder the smaller children near the fire perspired freely in zero weather, while the bigger boys on the other side of the room shivered with cold.

Swinging his lunch-box on the end of a strap, Noah

Webster walked four miles each morning to answer the schoolbell. Inside the bare building he took his place on a wooden bench, battered and scarred with aimless carving. The teacher—who taught every class—sat at a high desk in the middle of the room.

A group of spellers was summoned to stand in front of him.

"Beelzebub," roared the teacher, whacking his desk with a ruler.

"B-e-e-l-z-e-b-u-b" shouted the more fortunate children. But those who stumbled or spelled it wrong received a whack with the ruler. In this way twenty hard words were absorbed in a morning.

The reading was done from a copy of the Psalter. Arithmetic problems came out of the teacher's head, and were copied into homemade notebooks to be worked out later. Pencils had been invented by that time, but no-one in West Hartford had seen one. The writing was all done with homemade ink and a quill pen, nothing more than a sharpened goose feather. Yet if the notebooks were blotchy, which they frequently were, the unlucky writer received a good rap on the knuckles with the ruler. All day long class followed class in this manner.

Since Noah had never seen any other kind of school, he took this kind of instruction for granted. Still, he found it unsatisfactory. So many questions occurred to him through the day, questions the teacher would not answer.

"Please, sir, where is Babylon?" he would ask during a pause in the reading.

The teacher glared at him. "That is no part of the lesson," he answered.

"Are there books which tell such things?" he persisted.

"That question you must ask of the minister. He is a man with books."

"But his books are written mostly in Latin. I can't read them."

"There is no need for you to read them. Only boys who are going to college need to know Latin. Here you may learn to cipher and spell. That is enough for a young bumpkin."

"But I like book-learning better than anything. I want to read—more and more."

"Too much reading is bad for a boy. You should know how to spell and read the Bible. Beyond that you need not go."

"There must be some way—" thought Noah. He would ask his mother about it.

His mother, however, could not help him. Education, she said, was very expensive. A farmer's son could not hope to get it. When she was next in Hartford she would try to get him a book from the Librarian Company. With that he must be satisfied.

It was not until spring of the new year that he got any real help with his problem. In April, however, a new minister came to the village church, a young man named

Nathan Perkins. Dr. Perkins had graduated from Princeton. He liked to sit by the fire reading after supper.

When Noah came timidly to see him one evening, he received him cordially.

"Come in, come in, my boy," he said. "Your father has been telling me about you. Perhaps I can lend you something to read."

Noah moistened his lips. "It is the Latin, I think, sir. Could a shaver like me learn Latin?"

"Well, now, he might. Why is it you want to learn Latin?"

"Only that so many books are written in that language. If I knew the meaning of the words, I could read them."

"A scholar then you would be!"

Gravely he studied the boy before him. Thin and wiry, with flaming blue eyes and thick, red hair, Noah did not look much like a scholar. His rough, homemade shoes dripped with water from the melting snow outside. His trousers of nankeen—a kind of brownish cotton cloth— were faded and shrunk from much washing.

"Aren't the men in your family all farmers?"

"Yes, sir. But I like to read and learn things. This winter is my last in school. The schoolmaster himself says he can no longer teach me."

"Well, now, that is a pity. Come, what do you make of this?"

He handed a book down from the shelf over the fireplace.

"Nothing much now, sir. But if I could take it home and tackle it—"

"A spunky lad, at any rate. Very well, take it home and let me know later what you think of it."

"One more question I would like to ax, sir."

"*Ask,* not *ax,* Noah."

"*Ask.* If a boy learns Greek and Latin—must he become a preacher?"

"Not necessarily. There are many kinds of educated men. Teachers and writers and lawyers. Would you like to become one of them?"

"Whichever *knows* the most, sir."

"*Whoever* knows the most, Noah."

"*Whoever,* then."

Buttoning his coat over the precious book, Noah bade the new minister goodnight.

The book which Dr. Perkins lent him was a Latin grammar. If the boy really wanted to learn, thought Dr. Perkins, he must learn first that knowledge does not come easily. Education was like the black walnuts which the boys gathered in the woods outside the village. To reach the sweet meat inside one must first crack the hard, black shell which protected it.

Novels and story-books were almost unknown in New

England at that time. There were none in the minister's library. His twenty or thirty-odd books contained sermons, essays in Latin, a volume or two by English authors. The essays of Alexander Pope were favorite reading with him. There were two lines from Pope that he was fond of quoting to himself, when he thought of boys like Noah Webster, who came announcing that they wished to learn more.

'Tis education forms the common mind
Like as the twig is bent, the tree's inclined.

If this boy really wanted to learn, he would teach him.

Meanwhile young Noah spent every moment he could with the precious grammar. The moments were few enough in the springtime. Too busy even to go to school, he plowed the long furrows in his father's fields behind a pair of oxen, dreaming of the time when he would no longer be a farmer.

The spring weather was exhilarating; it filled a boy with ambition. In the trees behind the house blackbirds were calling. The orchard had burst into bloom—a cloud of pink and white blossoms.

On a day when the sky was full of scudding gray clouds, Noah flung down his plow and sought his father. The father was mending harness in the shed. Patiently he bent over the pieces of leather.

"Father!" cried Noah. "I have something to tell ye. I must have more learning!"

"But, Son!" protested the father. "Schooling costs money. And where is the money to come from? The farm feeds and clothes us, but it doesn't provide much money. How could I pay your school bills? How can I farm without ye?"

Crestfallen, the boy crept back to his plowing.

That evening he went again to see Dr. Perkins. Dr. Perkins looked sober.

"It is true, my boy, that schooling costs money. I can prepare you for college for a small sum, but you must realize that college would cost nearly thirty pounds a year for four years."

"That's almost one hundred and fifty Spanish dollars, isn't it?" gasped Noah, remembering that the village school cost his father only five shillings and a load of firewood every year.

"Yes it is, my boy. We must think twice before suggesting that your father send you to college."

"And yet where else would I go to read books and learn things?" asked Noah bitterly. "There are twenty-five hundred books in the library at Yale College. The other preacher was a-telling me."

"Perhaps your father could borrow the money," said Dr. Perkins slowly. "And let you pay him back later. That is, if you are really serious about studying. It would not do to spend the money, if you have no steady purpose."

"Oh, I would study every minute," cried Noah. "And

when I was finished and earning, I would pay back every penny to my father."

"I will talk to him about it. But first let me see how you are getting on with the grammar."

He took the book from Noah, and heard him recite several lessons. Noah did not pronounce the words properly, but he knew all the rules by heart. There was no doubting his determination.

All through the long summer of 1772 Noah worked doggedly at the grammar. He must show Dr. Perkins— and his father. Coming up from the fields at noontime, he stretched himself under a tree in the orchard, forgetting his dinner, waiting inside, forgetting the corn waiting also. Seeing him lying there with his book, his father looked very thoughtful.

If he mortgaged the farm, he could perhaps raise the money to send Noah to college. The four other children in the family showed no desire for advanced study. One preacher or doctor or lawyer in the family would be a good thing. Dr. Perkins said Noah had a good mind, worth developing.

The boy did not have the body of a farmer. Thin and quick-moving and talkative, he could do a day's work as well as anyone, but his talent seemed to lie elsewhere. His "stick-to-it-iveness" was extraordinary. When he wanted to do something, he plunged at it with the determination to move mountains.

When he spoke to his wife about sending Noah to

"Father!" cried Noah Webster. *"I want to go to Yale College."*

college, Mrs. Webster said Noah seemed smart enough, but did not eat properly! He ought to be fatter!

And yet hearing him whistle the Yankee Song out in the woodshed, she was forced to admit that the lad had plenty of "sperit." She would make dumplings for dinner tomorrow, instead of the usual hasty pudding. Perhaps he would like that better.

CHAPTER FIVE

Tea Is Spilt in Boston

IN THE FALL Noah began to go regularly each day to Dr. Perkins for lessons.

At that time there were few regular preparatory schools for college. True, there was in each county some kind of "academy" offering instruction in Latin and Greek. At Hartford the Hopkins Grammar School filled this purpose. A great many of the boys, however, went to their local ministers for lessons, rather than take the long horseback ride into town to school each day. If there were only one horse in the stable, this might almost be necessary.

Sometimes there were two horses in the Webster stable, sometimes only one, beside the span of oxen which did the plowing. Whatever the number that winter of 1772, Noah was glad to go to Dr. Perkins for his lessons. The work consisted chiefly in learning to read and write Greek and Latin. That knowledge alone, with a letter from Dr. Perkins, would get him into Yale in the fall of 1774, when he hoped to be ready.

As a student, Noah was a natural learner. His mind was like lightning. In the words of Robert Louis Stevenson, describing himself nearly a hundred years later, he "drank up books like water and was the better for it." Robert Louis Stevenson, however, really had books. Noah merely read earnestly in two or three of the minister's volumes, and put them carefully back on the shelf. The fact that so few books had been brought out from England, and none at all published in the Colonies, remained in his mind.

The following winter, Dr. Perkins being busier than usual, he tried the Grammar School in Hartford. The building there was nice—brick, with a good wood stove instead of an open fireplace. The teaching, however, was mediocre. Most of the boys preparing in Hartford would go to Yale, and Yale was one of the least flourishing of the nine American colleges. Whether the building was of brick or wood, no-one seemed to care very much what went on there. No-one but young Noah Webster, now fifteen years old and hoping to be ready for college by his sixteenth birthday. Knowing that his father was farming without him, and that the farm would have to be mortgaged to pay for his education, he felt in some haste to get ready. Besides, there burned in his head like a candle the thought of the twenty-five hundred books in the Yale library. Surely in such a mass of printing he would find the answers to all his questions.

Meanwhile, his old interest in the affairs of the Colonies had not abated. Neither did Colonial affairs stand still. During the winter that he studied in Hartford good news and bad came in with every post. The men who carried the mailbags on smoothly-trotting small horses were welcomed in every village.

The people of Boston, it seems, had decided not to accept tea with even a small duty placed on it. When three shiploads of it arrived in November and early December, they refused to let it be landed. The local police force of Boston consisted of a sheriff and a night watchman who cried the hours up and down the streets at night. Any real disturbance must be handled by the British soldiers—the "lobsters."

No-one wanted any disturbance, of course. They merely wanted to demonstrate that there must be "no taxation without representation." So on the night of December 16, 1773, a strange band of "Indians" made their way silently to Griffin's Wharf, where the ships lay. Probably one hundred and fifty "Indians," accompanied by several thousand not-so-silent townspeople. Quickly boarding the first ship, and demanding keys and lights from the mate, the "Indians" began to open chests of tea and throw the contents overboard into the water. Hour after hour the work went on. There were over three hundred chests of tea on the three ships; the cargo was worth £20,000, or nearly $100,000. By morning a fine odor of tea mingled with the salt breeze coming from the harbor. It was a breeze worth a fortune, as the indignant Englishmen saw it. To the Americans chuckling on the dark wharf it was worth even more—as a measure of Yankee determination.

The boys in the Grammar School in Hartford, and everyone else throughout the Colonies, read the story of the "Boston Tea Party" in their local newspapers. Details not included in the newspaper traveled by word of mouth.

"Listen, have ye heard the latest?" cried one boy to another as they reached the school in the morning. "A man came home after the Tea Party in Indian dress, and frightened his own children something awful."

"There were tea in all their shoes. The womenfolk got up early to sweep the doorsteps."

"A man named Paul Revere helped to do it. There is a song about him."

The boy telling the news struck up a fine falsetto.

> Rally, Mohawks! bring out your axes
> And tell King George we'll pay no taxes
> On his foreign tea;
>
> * * *
>
> Our Warren's there and bold Revere
> With hands to do, and words to cheer
> For Liberty and laws.

There was more to the song, but the boy singing it could not remember the words. This made no difference to the boys. It was enough for them to know that men like Paul Revere existed. Noah Webster, who liked to sing, was soon bawling a fragment of the new song with the others.

But of course throwing the tea into the water did not

end the affair in Boston. In June came orders directly from England, closing the port of Boston to all shipping until the stolen tea was paid for. Since Boston was chiefly a sea-port this meant the ruin of all her business. She might even go hungry, since supplies came largely by sea to her people.

Still, no-one intended to pay for the tea. Instead, all the thirteen Colonies sent delegates to Philadelphia in the late summer to a Congress to discuss the matter. This company of fifty-six men prepared a handsome petition to the King of England, asking that the duty on tea—and the soldiers!—be removed from Boston. Even more handsome than the petition were the lavish dinners served by the people of Philadelphia to the delegates. Turtle and trifle and gooseberry fool, twenty kinds of candy, called sweetmeats, fruits and almonds, appeared on the tables. The good Quakers of Philadelphia had a reputation for hospitality.

Meanwhile the people of Boston were not forgotten. As the summer advanced, there came pouring into Boston by land great carts of provisions from the other Colonies. Rye and codfish and cattle. Cornmeal and potatoes. A flock of live sheep from Connecticut. Not a man went hungry. Five thousand soldiers were now in Boston, yet they dared not leave the city itself, so hostile was the country round about. It was merely a matter of time before the teakettle set boiling in the cold waters of Boston Bay would boil over completely.

While it was still simmering uneasily, people settled back a little into their old ways. Noah Webster, having finished his work at the Grammar School, went back to Dr. Perkins for a summer of hard work. He was now almost sixteen years old. In September, when Yale opened for the fall term, he meant to be there as a member of the freshman class.

CHAPTER SIX

To College on Horseback

YALE COLLEGE IN the year 1774 consisted of three shabby brick buildings in the old town of New Haven on the shore of Long Island Sound. The town itself was lovely with its fine old trees and air of quiet dignity.

Packing to go to this institution on a crisp morning in September, Noah thought it the most exciting day in his whole life. How his tongue wagged as he folded his new suit and surtout—a tight-fitting, longish overcoat, cut down from his father's. For the journey itself he would wear his old clothes, since he must walk practically the whole thirty-five miles beside his father's horse.

The clothing was packed into the saddle-bags on the horse's back, along with some thick pork sandwiches and cold cornbread. A jug of cider, also strapped to the saddle, would quench their thirst during the journey. Noah would rather have had milk, but he knew it would turn to butter long before they reached New Haven.

On the worn doorstep of the red farmhouse, his mother stood waiting to say good-by to him. Dr. Perkins was there, too, smiling and holding his hat in his hands. **Mrs.** Webster's fingers trembled as she twisted the hem of her apron nervously. This fourth child of hers, with the fresh cheeks and sandy hair, was young to be going out alone into the world. True, the life at New Haven would be anything but free and untrammeled. Besides, she could trust her Noah. But who would see that he changed his stockings regularly, and ate enough meat for dinner? Without her warning voice, he might not go in to dinner at all.

Before climbing into the saddle, the father stood with the boy and his mother on the doorstep.

"Good-by and God keep you, my son," said Noah's mother. "Remember, we wish you to do good in the world and to be useful. Try to win the approval of all the good people you meet."

It was a solemn farewell, and made a deep impression on Noah.

All day the horse plodded along the road, carrying the father while the boy walked. Occasionally they changed places, so that Noah might rest for an hour in the saddle, but most of the way he walked, since it was only fitting that his father do most of the riding.

Just as the sun was setting, they arrived in New Haven. With an eye long accustomed to seeing Yale in his dreams, Noah looked for the first time at the College. Those three plain brick buildings. In which one would he sleep, where eat, and where recite his lessons? Like any Freshman, he must ask his way. An obliging Senior in a black gown directed them.

"That building there with the steeple is the chapel. The library's there, too, and a lot of stuffed birds and such. Over there's Connecticut Hall: you sleep and study there. The blue building's where we go for classes and victuals. There's a buttery there, where you can buy sweetmeats and cakes and beer and metheglin."

Noah knew the drink, called metheglin, made of honey and water, but he also knew that his father's worn purse held little more than the thirty pounds necessary for his board and tuition. "I won't be buying much at the buttery," he said nervously. "I don't figure on doing much spending."

"Not too much hard money, eh?" answered the Senior cheerfully. "Most of the lads here are like that."

"Ye ought to get along here then, Son," put in Mr. Webster. "Now you go and find your room, while I see about paying over the money. I'll feel freer once I get rid of these notes."

The notes to which he referred were the thirty British pounds he had brought with him.

The next morning Noah plunged fully into the life of the college. There were forty boys, he discovered, in the freshman class, one hundred and fifty students altogether. All the classes were conducted in Latin: the boys must write and recite in this dead language.

As the year went on, he came to like this arrangement

better and better. You could say exactly what you meant in Latin, much more so than in English. Every word had its exact meaning and its own place in the sentence. Impossible to use words carelessly. How he blushed to remember that at home he once said "ax" for "ask" or "chimbley" for "chimney."

Life itself at the college was not at all formal. Indeed at times it was distinctly crude. For breakfast the boys went to the college buttery for bread and butter and coffee. Dinner was served at long tables in the dining-hall beneath a sort of platform where the five members of the faculty sat together. At each table a single can of cider went from hand to hand—up one side and down another. The menu was all too familiar. Still the broth with the ball of cornmeal in it, called Injun pudding. Then boiled meat, potatoes, and cabbage, or turnips or dandelion greens instead of the cabbage. The meat was not always very tender.

Sometimes a piece of this tough meat, or a chunk of bread, flew mysteriously across the room, catching an unsuspecting student on the head or shoulder. The freshmen particularly received these unexpected morsels.

There were other ways, too, in which the freshmen were made to feel their inferiority. They alone wore no academic gowns, usually running hatless through the streets in their oldest clothes. At all times they must wait on the three upper classmen, greasing their boots, running their errands.

The acting president of the college, really the professor of divinity, and the one other full professor, always wore black robes, white wigs and high cocked hats. The three tutors who assisted them wore silk gowns. The boys themselves, however, even the upper classmen in flying black robes, made no effort to be dignified. It was a shock to young Noah Webster, taught to regard Yale as a fountain of solemn behavior.

Other things about the college were puzzling, too. The blue recitation hall where they attended classes, for instance, was distinctly rickety and musty. Many of the books in the library were dusty beyond belief. Had no-one, then, been reading them lately? Were they not quite a gold-mine of wonderful knowledge? Truth to tell, some of the books were quite beyond reading, and others did not seem to have much bearing on the work he was doing. Still, with several thousand to choose from he would surely find there all that he wished to know. Bravely he pressed on with his reading.

Supper after the day's work was, as always, his favorite meal. The familiar rye bread and milk, with baked apples or a little "relish," supplied all that he needed. After supper there was usually a good deal of laughing, talking and singing. Noah was not a boy who laughed easily. The Yankee farm-lads seldom did. But he could talk and argue with the best of them!

In music, too, he more than held his own. He had learned to play the fife lately, an instrument like a flute which carried the tune for a dozen singers. The fife-player led the singing; the others merely followed.

Sometimes the boys at Yale laughed at Noah Webster, because he was always so willing to step forward and become the leader in anything. They tried to think of a name which would describe his eager manner. Some said he was like a little general, taking charge of whatever was going on. Others said he was a walking question-mark. Still others said that he was the brightest boy in the freshman class; someday Yale would be proud of him.

The songs, which the boys sang and played, were full of melody and spirit. In the fife and drum corps there were three favorites: *My Dog and Gun, On the Road to Boston,* and the *Yankee Song. My Dog and Gun* reminded the boys of wet autumn days, when they had poked around the woods at home, in search of pheasants or rabbits.

New words for the old songs were soon to be written, however. New songs themselves, too. As early as 1768 someone had published in a Boston newspaper new words for the old English air, *Hearts of Oak.* The new words were called *The Liberty Song.* The first verse began, "Come join hand in hand, brave Americans all." The people of the Colonies felt more and more that they must join hand in hand to do something about preserving their liberty.

Believing that war might come, the good people of Massachusetts had begun to collect powder and shot in secret places. A few old cannon were collected and oiled. The men on the farms took down their long muskets, which they used in winter-time to shoot squirrels and ducks, and cleaned and oiled them.

Feverishly at night in their rooms the boys at Yale discussed the fate of the American Colonies.

"There be 'redcoats' landing in New York as well as in Boston," said one lad. "If the two armies march at the same time, we'll be squeezed like a nut in a nutcracker here in Connecticut."

"Well, if war comes, I shall enlist!" said another boy, poking the fire fiercely.

"If you can find the army!" said another. "The Colonies have no sojers or cannon or money or anything."

"There's the militia in every town," retorted the other. "My father's a member already."

"It'll take some doing to turn the militia into an army," said the other. "Besides, a shaver like you couldn't fight. They'd have you cleaning mules in no time."

Noah, who was himself small for his age, and rather peaked with much studying, thought it was time to enter the conversation.

"Big or little, our fathers fought plenty against the Indians, when they were young. We can do the same."

"Indians, yes! But these British soldiers are different. There are thousands of them, and they have guns and cannon and everything."

"Everything but the sure knowledge of a just cause,"

said Noah quietly. "Lots of people in England think the American Colonies are right. They'd be on our side."

"On our side three thousand miles away!" jeered the other boy. "I tell you we couldn't do it."

"Maybe not," said Noah. "But if worse come to worst, we can try anyway."

At this moment a monitor came fussing at the door.

"Boys, boys," he said. "There's too much noise here. It's time for lights out. All of you who don't belong here go to your rooms. Mr. Buckminster doesn't like noise."

Mr. Buckminster was the tutor in charge of all the freshmen. Like a shepherd with a flock of sheep, he heard all their lessons and prayed over them when they misbehaved. The boys did not like Mr. Buckminster, but they did not pay much attention to him. Strong leaders were lacking in Yale at that time. Noah Webster, however, who was one of the youngest freshmen, thought everyone should do just as Mr. Buckminster said. Unlike some of the other boys, he could not take college lightly. He was a Yankee farm-lad, going to Yale on borrowed money.

CHAPTER SEVEN

The Man on Horseback

NEWS OF IMPORTANCE, which reached New Haven by the morning post, was thundered at the students in chapel by Dr. Daggett. On Friday morning, the twenty-first of April, 1775, there was news indeed.

War, Dr. Daggett said, had come! Some American farmers had fought with British soldiers the preceding Wednesday near Boston!

Breathlessly, the boys listened to the story. On Tuesday night a group of eight hundred soldiers set out from Boston at midnight to march to Concord, eighteen miles away. Rowing across the Charles River, and wading ashore in the cold April moonlight, they began their journey. Advance scouts had told them of certain stores hidden at Concord—sacks of flour and bullets, guns and cannon as well. They knew exactly where the stores were; it should be a simple matter to capture them. Elaborate precautions had been taken to see that no-one rode out from Boston that night to warn the people of Concord that they were coming. The road across Boston Neck, on the south, which connected the city with the mainland, was well guarded. Further inland there were more soldiers. A warship with sixty-seven guns lay in the river north of the city, to prevent anyone crossing to Charlestown and carrying a message that way.

And yet when the soldiers marched into Lexington at dawn, a good twelve miles from their starting point, they found sixty or seventy farmers, armed with muskets, drawn up on the Green to meet them. The leader of the soldiers, Major Pitcairn, saw that he must act and act quickly.

"Disperse, ye rebels, disperse! Lay down your arms!" he shouted.

Not a man laid down his musket. Instead, from somewhere a single shot rang out. The next moment the soldiers fired a volley at the defiant farmers. Eight men fell dead, and another ten were wounded. The rest of the men scattered hastily.

Marching on toward Concord, six miles distant, the soldiers found the whole countryside awake and aware of their coming. Bells rang out, drums beat the call to arms. When they got within a short distance of the village another group of armed farmers met them. But these men did not stand in ranks waiting to be slaughtered. They faced about, and piped the soldiers into the village with fife and drum. The situation looked brighter.

Reaching the tavern in the Square, the soldiers relaxed and demanded breakfast. While the officers sprawled at ease, small groups of their men went after the stores.

Strangely enough, they did not find many. A farmer, plowing in a field, did not tell them there were cannon buried under the new furrow. A woman bending over a barrel of soap did not say that she was hiding the church silver there. Fresh wagon tracks into a nearby swamp did not suggest to anyone that kegs of powder, cannon balls, and sacks of bullets, had been carried there hastily three days before, by a group of men and boys working feverishly with their ox-carts.

The few sacks of flour and bullets, which the soldiers did find, they threw into a creek. Then they came back to the Square.

Word came that a group of rebels was gathered on the far side of a bridge north of the village. A small detachment went to investigate. The officers sitting about the Square heard unexpected shots, then the familiar volley, which meant that the soldiers had fired. But this time that did not end the matter, as it had at Lexington. There were more shots—apparently the farmers had not scattered. When reinforcements were sent to the bridge, they found the soldiers retreating in some disorder, leaving half their officers on the ground behind them.

The situation did not now look so bright. As the day advanced it grew steadily worse. Reinforcements from Boston failed to arrive. It became hourly more dangerous to remain in Concord. Thousands of men apparently were pouring into the village.

All of these men carried muskets. Some of them carried

a few comforts as well, cornbread and an extra pair of stockings, perhaps, tied up in a pillow-case. The pillow-cases made them look slightly ridiculous, but none of the British soldiers laughed. Instead their officers decided that they must begin the march back to Boston immediately.

The first four miles of that march were a terrible ordeal for the soldiers. From behind barns and stone walls, trees and farmhouses, came a steady stream of bullets. Scores of soldiers were killed; many others were wounded. It was plain that these Yankee farmers did not like having eighteen of their number killed or wounded as they stood on the Green at Lexington earlier in the day.

How, then, had the farmers known that the soldiers were coming? It was long before the soldiers discovered, but the people of the Colonies knew almost immediately. Dr. Daggett in his pulpit was able to tell most of the story. Further details came with every post.

It seems that the good people of Boston had prepared well for just this emergency. Should the soldiers march, two men were ready to try to get out of the city to warn the countryside that "the regulars are coming." One would ride out over the Neck, hoping to slip through the sentries there. Another would row over to Charlestown, if possible, in the teeth of the warship, and from there start on horseback to warn the people. A boy with two lanterns would hang one or two in the belfry of old North Church, depending on whether they were marching by land or taking boats across the river to Cambridge.

The man chosen to row across to Charlestown, and from there ride inland, was none other than Paul Revere, the silversmith, who had helped throw the tea into the harbor. His boat already lay hidden at an obscure wharf. In Charlestown a certain Mr. Larkin had an excellent horse waiting.

Riding out with information was not new to Paul Revere. Only the preceding Sunday, he had ridden to Concord in the daytime, to warn the people there to hide their stores. Certain gossip in the stables, the sight of many soldiers polishing their boots and brushing their uniforms on Saturday, made it seem certain that they were going out soon, either to capture the stores at Concord, or to arrest two men hidden at Lexington, who were known to be urging the farmers to resist the soldiers.

In peaceful times Paul Revere spent long hours at his bench, wearing a leather apron while he made silver mugs and teapots. On the night of Tuesday, April the eighteenth, however, he was waiting at home for a message. At ten o'clock a man knocked at his door, saying he must start at once: the soldiers were already drawn up on the Common.

Hurrying in some excitement to the place where his boat lay, Revere forgot to take with him both his spurs and some pieces of flannel to muffle the oars while he was rowing. Neither of the two men, who would row with him, thought of the flannel either. There was no time to go back home for it, but one of the men remembered

On Mr. Larkin's good brown horse Revere set off for Lexington.

a girl who lived nearby. Whistling softly under her window, he got her to throw down a flannel petticoat, still warm from her body.

There remained now the problem of the spurs. Revere wrote a note to his wife, tied it on his dog's collar, and ordered the animal home. In a few minutes he was back, the spurs tied securely where the note had been.

Cautiously the three men lowered the boat into the water. Then more cautiously, stroke by stroke, they rowed in a wide circle around the threatening warship and reached Charlestown safely.

On Mr. Larkin's good brown horse Revere set off for Lexington. A short way up the road he saw soldiers standing under a tree. The soldiers gave chase, but, riding cross-country to another road, he out-distanced them. By midnight he was in Lexington, warning John Hancock and Sam Adams, the rebel leaders. By the time the soldiers reached Lexington at dawn, and stood facing the armed farmers on the Green, he was innocently carrying a leather trunk across the Square to the parson's house. The trunk contained all of John Hancock's papers, enough evidence to hang a dozen men for treason. It is still in existence today in a museum at Worcester, Massachusetts.

Once the trunk was in a safe place, Paul Revere went on about his business, which was to ride on to Concord. He never reached there, for he was captured en route and his horse taken away from him, but another man riding with him escaped and did arrive. Not one step of the way did the soldiers march that long night without finding everyone along the way fully aware of their movements. . . .

"Well!" said Noah Webster, when he heard the story. "Perhaps *now* the government in England will realize that the Colonists meant what they said when they asked for 'No taxation without representation!' "

All the rest of the day, he tried to study his lessons. But he could not put his mind on his work. The sound of gunfire was in his ears, although he was many miles from Boston. The thought of Paul Revere riding through the night filled him with awe and admiration.

Questions buzzed in his head like bees:

Could the American farmers really defeat the British army, if they organized for battle?

Why had the government at home been so stupid in this matter?

Could the Colonies get along without the protection of the mother country, if they declared their independence?

Could the people of America learn to make their own glass and silk—and books?

Where would his father and other men sell their pork and tobacco, if the English refused to buy it?

That day, at least, Noah was certainly a walking question-mark. Even after he fell asleep at night, he continued to ask himself questions he could not answer, in his dreams.

CHAPTER EIGHT

Yankee Doodle in Town

NOW THAT THE war was begun, the people of Massachusetts waited breathlessly to see if the twelve other Colonies would back them up in their argument with England. They did.

Over in New York State groups of local militia seized Fort Ticonderoga and other forts, well stocked with food and ammunition. Men from all the surrounding Colonies rode into Massachusetts to join the ragged horde, which was trying to keep the British bottled up in Boston.

Meanwhile in Philadelphia, so Dr. Daggett announced from his pulpit at New Haven, a second Continental Congress had assembled. This was no mere polite assembly, wishing to write letters to the King. It was a group of determined patriots ready to organize the War of Independence at considerable risk to their own necks. Every resolution they passed, of course, was an act of open rebellion against the lawful government of the country. Nevertheless, the resolutions came thick and fast during the weeks which followed.

After noting briefly in their opening session that the King had not answered their former petition, the delegates at the Congress voted to raise ten companies of three thousand men each to go to Boston. These men would know how to shoot with deadly accuracy. Their marching might not be very good, for none of them had had much practice. Their uniforms would be anything at all that could be scraped up in a hurry to cover the emergency. After all the new Congress had no money, no authority, no supplies, no experience. What it did have was a strong feeling that a new nation was being born on the American continent.

As leader for the new army, they chose a man named George Washington, a tobacco-planter from Virginia who had fought bravely in the French and Indian Wars. Mr. Washington was known to be determined and vigorous. In his own country he could out-ride and out-shoot any man for miles around. With a company of picked Virginia men he would start north immediately, gathering up other companies as he went. It was a good beginning for an American army.

In the meantime at Boston there had been a second bloody battle. A company of Yankees under Captain Prescott had decided to fortify a hill in Charlestown across the river from Boston. This hill, called Bunker Hill, had an excellent view of the city.

As soon as they heard of the new fortifications, of course, the British soldiers marched out to destroy them. Twice they charged the hill, but were beaten back with heavy losses. The third time they charged not a gun was fired at them.

The reason for this soon became apparent. The Yankee soldiers had run out of ammunition. Sixty kegs of powder, brought in successfully from the Concord swamps, were used during the first two sallies. During the third the men could only stand helplessly by, while the British soldiers took over their fortifications.

Yet these perverse American farmers were elated over the whole engagement. They had stood off a regular army as long as their ammunition lasted. As soon as they could collect more ammunition and more soldiers they would tackle this regular army again.

"This man Washington now, who's on his way up from Virginia," they said to each other, "once he gits here, we'll make things hot for them British 'lobsters'! By gum, it roils a man to hev his comrades shot down like so many turkeys on Lexington Green."

So the talk ran around the campfires in the evening—small fires for a warm night, where a man might fry a bit of fat pork or a brace of eggs, if he were lucky enough to have them. The farmers round about had done their best, but there were many empty bellies in this new Yankee army. If General Washington could do something about the lack of victuals as well as the shortage of ammunition, he would prove himself a great general!

Meanwhile the boys in New Haven had given up practically all pretense of studying. Dr. Daggett himself seemed to breathe out patriotism with every breath. His sermons on Sunday rang with the words liberty and independence. "The most important contest that has taken place on the globe for many centuries past" he said in discussing the War. Beside these fiery words the study of the Greek testament, logic and arithmetic seemed pale indeed.

Imbued with the military spirit, the boys had already formed their own company of militia at New Haven. A fife-and-drum corps led them through all their maneuvers. And who should march at the head of this musical unit but young Noah Webster, the voluble freshman with the bushy hair, who played the fife with such spirit? If his mother could have seen him then, she would have given up her strong conviction that no boy could play his part satisfactorily in this world without swallowing a liberal portion of Injun pudding every day. At sixteen Noah Webster led the fife-and-drum corps of Yale College very gallantly.

With great relish one morning Dr. Daggett announced that the new General Washington would pass directly through New Haven on his way north, and that the boys in the college company might pay their respects to him. If he stayed overnight, they might even escort him out of town the next morning as far as the village of Neckbridge.

It was a fine evening in June when General Washington rode into New Haven to spend the night. It was a fine morning when he rode out again to the music of the Yale fife-and-drum corps, playing the *Yankee Song:*

> There was a man in our town
> I pity his condition—

The words had no meaning for a general going forth to war, but the tune was invigorating.

Within a few months new words for the old tune were being improvised all over the country.

> Brother Ephraim sold his cow
> And bought him a commission—
>
> A Yankee boy is straight and tall,
> And never overfat, sir—
>
> Father and I went down to camp
> Along with Captain Goodwin,
> And there we saw the men and boys
> A-eating hasty pudding.
>
> Yankee Doodle went to town
> A-riding on a pony,
> Stuck a feather in his cap
> And called it macaroni.

Before the War of Independence was over, this song had become as much a part of American life as the Stars and Stripes are today.

CHAPTER NINE

The First Fourth of July

DURING THE SUMMER which followed Noah worked faithfully on his father's farm in West Hartford. The hay crop that year was enormous on account of an early spring. Load after load of the sweet-smelling dry grass went into the big barn, and still other loads remained. There was no end to the task.

After the hay was cut, there were the corn and tobacco to harvest. Then with the first crisp days of fall came barrel after barrel of apples to be picked and stored for the winter, or pressed into pungent cider.

For the fall butchering Noah could not stay. Young Charles at thirteen must help his father as best he could to prepare the winter's stock of ham and bacon, salt pork and sausage and lard. Abram, the big brother, was not at home either, for he had joined the army.

Noah was not sorry to miss the butchering, but he did hate to leave home with the hunting season coming on. In November wild ducks flew over every swamp, and the woods were full of plump squirrels and pheasants and rabbits. The first cloudy morning in November usually found the boys out at daybreak for a long ramble with their dogs and guns.

The college boys, of course, could not hope to hunt in the autumn. The six o'clock rising bell got them up for a brief breakfast, and chapel, and a long day at their books. The subjects they studied were not very lively either. Everyone took divinity, whether he intended to become a minister or not. Every Sophomore also studied Greek and Latin, geometry and geography. There was no history, no science, no literature, no sociology. Shakespere's plays had been written but they did not read them at Yale. Only the great, distant past of Greece and Rome was spread before them.

Small wonder, then, that the students followed the war so keenly. The remote past was over and done with. The present and future of America was in the making. News was scarce, but whenever one boy met another he asked eagerly, "What's acting?" By this question he meant, "What is happening?" It was the eternal question in every mind.

The situation in Boston had not changed much during the last eight months. Apparently the Yankees had the redcoats well bottled up in the city, but they did not have the gunpowder to blow them out of it. Desperate efforts to make the powder were, of course, being made, for conditions in Boston were deplorable. Houses were being pulled down for firewood, food was scarce, people were ill of smallpox and other diseases.

Yet the new General Washington was not idle. While everyone at home worried and fussed and wondered through the winter, certain of his officers were dragging cannon by ox-cart through the snow from New York State. These cannon, mounted in March on the hills of Dorchester overlooking the city, meant that the British soldiers must leave Boston at once. They did this hastily by boat on the seventeenth of March. It was General Washington's first victory.

Meanwhile in Philadelphia, so the boys heard, the Continental Congress had not been idle either. During that first year of the war the delegates to the Congress worked feverishly to set some kind of government in motion. In June, 1775, they voted to print two million Spanish dollars with which to pay their soldiers. In July they began to import muskets and gunpowder from Spain and France. A week later they set up a kind of postal service, with Benjamin Franklin, the publisher, as postmaster. In September they organized a small fleet. And through it all there were the pressing problems of the army: how to feed, clothe, shelter and doctor the men who were in the field fighting.

By April, 1776, more and more people were urging the Congress also to make some kind of formal declaration regarding American independence. Absurd to think and act as a new nation, without announcing one's existence. The world must be told in fitting terms just what was happening on the American continent.

And so for many days a man, named Thomas Jefferson, sat alone with pen and paper, writing a formal statement that the "United Colonies" were now "Free and Independent States." On the fourth of July, 1776, this statement was adopted by the Continental Congress.

News of its adoption could not be telephoned or wired to other cities, because there were no telephones or telegraph wires. Instead it traveled on horseback from one town to another. It was on July eighth that the news reached New Haven. Solemnly, with a pause after each sentence, Dr. Daggett read the Declaration in chapel.

When in the Course of human events, it becomes necessary for one people to dissolve the political Bands which have connected them with another, and to assume among the Powers of the earth, the separate and equal station to which the Laws of Nature and of Nature's God entitle them, a decent respect to the opinions of mankind requires that they should declare the causes which impel them to the separation.

We hold these truths to be self-evident, that all men are created equal, that they are endowed by their Creator with certain inalienable Rights, that among these are Life, Liberty, and the pursuit of Happiness. That to secure these rights, Governments are instituted among Men, deriving their just powers from the consent of the governed. That whenever any Form of Government becomes destructive of these ends, it is the Right of the People to alter or to abolish it, and to institute new Government, laying its foundation on such principles and organizing its powers in such form, as to them shall seem most likely to effect their Safety and Happiness.

The rest of the day was not as solemn as the reading in chapel. Along with everyone else in New Haven, the boys went wild. Bells rang. Guns were fired off. There were parades all day and a huge bonfire far into the night. Thus it was that the first Fourth of July was celebrated triumphantly in New Haven four days late.

The reading of the Declaration of Independence thrilled Noah Webster as much as had the Battle of Lexington. Until that time he had not thought so much about the Congress in Philadelphia. Now he was consumed with curiosity about the fifty-six men, who were delegates to it. *Who* were they, and *what* were they?

Sam Adams of Massachusetts he knew to be a brewer. John Hancock, also of Massachusetts, was a merchant. The Connecticut delegates were Samuel Huntington and Roger Sherman. Huntington, he knew, was a judge and Sherman a lawyer.

In a small way, of course, Noah's own father was a judge also—justice-of-the-peace for the village of West Hartford. People called him Judge Webster, but for every hour he sat indoors, settling small disputes or legal matters, he was outdoors a hundred in all weathers, taking care of his farm. Shrewd and silent, he found the life of a farmer satisfactory in many ways.

To young Noah, however, the life of a farmer was unsatisfactory, if only because it furnished so little opportunity to *talk*. Bursting with opinion on every subject, he could not get up much of an argument with the cows and oxen on his father's farm. One great luxury at Yale, where the food was poor and the rooms plain, was that there was always someone with whom he could talk.

The Continental Congress at Philadelphia seemed to him to offer a rare opportunity for men to get together and state their opinions freely. The work they did was fully as important, if not quite so heroic, as that of the soldiers. Who, then, were those men with the silver tongues, making decisions for all the Colonies and saying why they did with such convincing eloquence?

Thomas Jefferson of Virginia—a lawyer. James Smith of Pennsylvania—a lawyer. Richard Stockton of New Jersey—a lawyer. Lawyer, lawyer, lawyer. Of the fifty-six men, known to be attending the Congress, fourteen were lawyers and twelve jurists, which was much the same thing.

Sometime during his second year at Yale Noah decided that he, too, must become a lawyer. This would require more studying after college, but he was not afraid of hard work with books. The only thing he was afraid of was that in the new nation forming around him he would not find his rightful place. It was a load off his shoulders to decide to follow the same profession as John Hancock, president of the Continental Congress at Philadelphia!

CHAPTER TEN

The Battle of Saratoga

THE NEXT TWO years were war years for Noah Webster and the rest of the American people. Although he was supposed to be doing his Junior and Senior work at Yale, Noah spent very little time at the college. The horse, which carried him and his father by turns the thirty-five miles to New Haven, was constantly on the road.

In August, 1776, Noah came home because there was an epidemic of typhoid fever in New Haven. In November he went back, only to have the college close again in a few weeks because the war was creeping close. In January he went back; six weeks later the boys were sent home again. Late in May the Junior class was called together in Glastonbury, Connecticut, not far from Hartford, for a short summer session. After that classes were in session only three months during the next nine.

One reason why the college could not remain long in session was because the steward could not get food for the boys. British troops had landed in New York City, and were laying waste the country for miles around. Another British army marching down the Hudson River from Canada, cut Connecticut off on the west. Meat was scarce; the supply of cornmeal and potatoes dwindled daily. There was no sugar for morning coffee anywhere. The farmers had begun to cut up cornstalks, crush them in the cider mills, and boil the juice down to a kind of syrup for sweetening.

The people of the new United States could not blind themselves to the fact that the war was going very badly indeed. From across the river in New Jersey, Washington struggled in vain to drive the British out of New York City as he had done in Boston. In the northern part of New York State, British troops took town after town. If the two British armies should march successfully north and south until they met they would cut the United States squarely in half.

At home on the Webster farm Noah heard these facts grimly. He was still too young to enlist in the regular army, excepting perhaps as a drummer. Nevertheless boys of seventeen and eighteen, and even younger, had begun to drill with the local militia—the men over forty-five, who stood ready to protect their villages if the need arose.

When Noah came home from Glastonbury in the summer of 1777, he enlisted at once in this band of volunteers. Under his own father as Captain, he and his younger brother, Charles, shouldered a gun daily on the village Green. Abram, the older brother, had already been more than a year in the American army.

During that year Abram had been home twice, with

tales of army life. Breathlessly Noah, at seventeen, and Charles, at thirteen, had listened to him the preceding summer, when he came home to recuperate from an attack of smallpox.

"Half the men," said Abram, "are ill from fever or dysentery. We sleep around anywheres—in barns, in empty houses. The mosquitoes eat us alive."

"Tell us more about the shooting," urged Charles.

"Funny thing about that," said Abram. "For every battle ye fight, ye spend a month o' Sundays bein' miser·able. If it ain't sickness, it's bein' hungry, and if it ain't colder than Christmas, it's hotter than blazes. 'Bout all a man can do is keep his mouth shut, hang on, and hope for the best."

"But you do get to shoot at the sojers sometimes, don't you?" asked Charles anxiously.

"Soldiers, not sojers, Charles," said Noah. He didn't mean to be critical, but so many words in the mouths of Yankee schoolboys were twisted out of all recognition.

"We sure do, when we have bullets and powder. Trouble is, the other fellow seems to have three times what we have, whenever we tackle him."

"But the right is on our side, that ought to give our men courage," said Noah.

Abram scratched his head quizzically. "Oh, we don't lack for sperit, or for sharp shootin' either. But when one of them cannon balls comes along, it don't stop to ask questions."

Mrs. Webster, who had been listening silently to the three boys, shook out her apron.

"That's enough talkin' for now," she said decisively. "You, Charles, bring me in an armful of wood. Noah, get the milk from the spring-house. I'm making dumplings for supper."

"I could eat a panful all myself, Ma," said Abram. "Seems like I'll never be full again since I had that fever."

"You come along into the kitchen and drink some milk. You still look like a picked chicken."

"More like a old billy-goat than a chicken. Chickens don't have whiskers," said young Charles.

"You be careful now," warned his brother. "Or you'll get too big for your breeches."

"He's that already," sighed his mother, taking the words literally instead of as a joke, as Abram meant them. "I declare all I do is make clothes for you boys. Abram didn't have a rag fit to be seen in, when he came home, and now Charles is popping out of his clothes."

"How about me? Don't I get some new trousers soon?" said Noah, coming in with the milk. "It's the seat of mine that gets worn through. The life of a student is hard on trousers."

"You'll all get a clout on the head, if you don't stop teasing me, and let me get the supper," answered Mrs. Webster. But she was happy to have her three sons at home together. It was not often that she had them thus.

That was the preceding summer. Now Abram was home again, deeply tanned from his life in the open, but so anxious about the war that he had no heart for joking. No-one had any heart for joking that summer. If Connecticut was squeezed between two armies, where would they all look for help?

One morning late in September, it seemed as if their worst fears were about to be realized. A man came riding along the road, stopping at every house to say that General Burgoyne's army was marching toward Albany, and other troops had started up the Hudson from New York City.

Men and boys of all ages began gathering on the Green. So rapidly did they come, they did not stop to change their sweat-stained shirts or pack a knapsack. Those who had muskets snatched them and ran. Those who lacked muskets grabbed up old swords or pistols, hayforks or hatchets as weapons. Charles, who was barely fifteen, and Noah, not yet nineteen, took their places beside their father and elder brother. They made a strange family group: the father, weathered and silent; Abram, red from the sun; Noah, pale from much study; young Charles, lively and active. Around them crowded neighbors of all ages.

A strenuous two days' march brought them within sight of the Hudson River. On the opposite bank lay the city of Kingston, afire and burning fiercely. The sight of it made them set their jaws more firmly.

Fifty miles north of Kingston lay Albany. Was General Burgoyne there already? Was it his advance guard which had fired Kingston? Wearily the amateur army pressed on.

A few miles further north a man, waving a sword, came riding to meet them.

"General Burgoyne has surrendered! We have taken his army prisoner at Saratoga!" he shouted.

The people of New England were saved. The war was not yet won, but it was not lost either. General Washington, down in New Jersey, might still lead his army to victory. The men with the pitchforks and old pistols could go home for yet another winter of painful uncertainty.

CHAPTER ELEVEN

The World Comes Closer

IN APRIL, 1778, a new president came to Yale, Dr.
Ezra Stiles. Dr. Stiles was a forceful man, who had
done a great many things in his lifetime—preached
to the Indians, studied law, taught science and divinity,
studied Oriental languages, made electrical experiments.
Now he was going to be president of Yale.

This being so, he thought the first thing to do was to
get the boys back to New Haven. Yes, there was a war
going on, but most of the students were too young to
fight in it. There was some danger of New Haven being
invaded by the enemy, but that danger existed in most of
their home towns and villages, too.

Meanwhile, the resources of the college were not
being used. Twenty-five hundred books in the library,
and no boys there to read them! The new Republic would
need educated men: Yale was there to supply them.

With a man like Dr. Stiles in charge, the boys soon
came hurrying back to New Haven. Dr. Stiles' first words
to them were bracing:

"Gentlemen," he said, "we have work to do here. I
do not wish to know if the enemy has marched through

your towns or burned your hayfields. I want to know how much Greek and Latin you have read during the past two years."

The steward reported that there was no sugar for the morning coffee.

"We will drink it plain—or not at all," said Dr. Stiles calmly. "Water will make an excellent substitute. It has always been a fine beverage. There is still plenty of it!"

Final examinations for the Senior class would begin in July. Since it was already June, they could see for themselves how busy they would be in the interval.

"Work is good for everyone!" he said emphatically. "It keeps young firebrands from burning too brightly!"

The boys rather liked being called young firebrands. Certainly it was better than being prayed over by Tutor Buckminster.

Again the campus rang with friendly greetings. How good it was, thought Noah, to be back with his friends, Joel Barlow and Ichabod Wetmore. The war had burned deeply into his consciousness; he would never forget the struggle for American independence. Dr. Stiles, however, made him realize that a war cannot be fought in a college dormitory. Those of the students who were ready for the army should go out and enlist in it. Those who remained must give their best attention to their books.

Probably at no time in his life did Noah see the summer pass with so little notice taken of it. Birds sang,

"Water," stated Dr. Stiles, "has always been a good beverage."

flowers bloomed. The lovely white houses and old trees of New Haven dozed in the sunshine. But the boys were wide-awake. To please this vigorous Dr. Stiles, who had preached to the Indians, they were willing to work inexhaustibly.

September came—the month for graduation. More than thirty boys graduated with Noah Webster in September. The exercises were conducted in Latin, but there was a history oration given in English. The student who made this important speech was young Mr. Webster, not quite twenty years old. Among the thirty-odd boys in his class, he stood well up toward the top when the final grades were posted.

The morning after graduation Noah set out with his father for West Hartford. Gravely the father insisted that Noah ride in the saddle.

"Ye are a man of learning now," he said. "'Tis fitting ye take the seat of honor."

"Oh, no, Father, I couldn't!"

"Take it, Son, take it. 'Tis little enough I can do to show my pride in you."

And so the boy rode—not all the way, but often.

Little was said on the way home, for father Webster seldom talked much. Noah, dreaming in the saddle, let the hours glide quietly by.

Toward evening the landscape grew more familiar, and at last they came to their own fields and the red farmhouse on the ridge. The smoke from the chimney was like a plume of welcome.

The next morning, however, Noah's father drew him into the worn parlor, and closed the door.

"The time has come, Son," he said, "to talk about the future."

"I know, Pa," said Noah. "I must not idle away the hours. If I am to be a lawyer, I must begin to read jurisprudence."

Mr. Webster looked thoughtful. "I was not thinking of that so much, Son—" he began.

Noah interrupted him. "If I work hard, perhaps I can pass my bar examinations in the spring or the fall anyway. When the war is over, I must be ready to take up practice."

"I was not thinking of *after* the war, Son," said Mr. Webster slowly. "I was thinking of *now,* this winter. You must find some work to do at once. In times like these it will not be easy."

"You mean—you don't want me to study law this winter, Pa!"

"I mean I have no money any more for anything. Probably I shall lose the farm before I finish."

"Lose the farm!" gasped Noah. "Because I went to college!"

"For that and other reasons. The country, Son, is in grave trouble. Our money no longer has any true value."

"I don't understand what you mean, Father."

Mr. Webster went on to explain. Money, he said, "hard" money, was growing scarce in the new Republic.

The war had ruined America's foreign trade. Therefore no English or French or Spanish money was coming into the country. Instead the government kept sending out what guineas and francs and Spanish dollars it could collect to buy arms and ammunition.

There must, however, be money of some sort for people to use. So the government printed paper money. But since there was no gold in the treasury to balance this, the paper money had no real value. Each day it shrank a little in value. As long as the Bank of England existed, a hundred pounds today would be worth a hundred pounds tomorrow. But where was the Bank of the United States, loaded with gold, to make five hundred American dollars today worth five hundred dollars tomorrow?

Instead, the money was like a snowball. A year ago an American dollar had been worth three English shillings and twopence. Today it was worth only one shilling. Tomorrow it would be worth even less. A man who owed a hundred and twenty English pounds, as Mr. Webster did for Noah's education, might have to pay his debt three or four times over, if he paid in American money. And yet whenever he sold a sheep, or sack of potatoes, he received American money for it.

"I hate to say it, Son," said Mr. Webster. "But the other boys have lost out through your going to college."

A fierce pang of remorse shot through young Noah.

"I didn't know, Pa," he said, "I'll never take another penny from you as long as I live."

Mr. Webster made a gesture of protest.

"I don't aim to turn ye out like an orphan, Son," he said. "But this is all I can do for ye." Reaching into his pocket, he drew out a crumpled bill, marked $8. Handing this to Noah, he said, "From now on ye must make your own way in the world."

For three days after the talk with his father, Noah remained upstairs in his bedroom. His mind was in a whirl. He had had no idea that a war brought with it such problems.

In many ways during the last few months the war had seemed to be going better. Only last month a fine fleet of French ships came to help the Yankees.

But now he knew that the war had ruined his father financially. His own future, too, seemed wiped out by the emergency.

Wildly he cast about for something he might do to earn a living. He might preach perhaps, if anyone wanted a minister barely twenty, but he felt no call to be a preacher. There were Indians who traveled from town to town in peacetime, selling medicine, but he was no Indian and he knew nothing about medicine. A tinker came through occasionally on a wagon, selling new pots and kettles, but tinkers were usually the worst kind of ignorant rascals.

He thought of his great-great-grandfather, pushing through the wilderness over a hundred years ago, and wondered what the old gentleman would have done under the circumstances. Then he thought of his mother with her supply of homely maxims to fit every occasion.

"Waste not, want not." She said that when her grandchildren did not clean up their plates at dinner.

"A stitch in time saves nine." She said that when young Charles did not want to stand still while she sewed a button on his coat.

"There is more than one way to skin a rabbit." She said that when she had to make suet pudding without raisins, or put four children to sleep crossways in a bed that was too crowded to use the customary way.

"The Lord helps them who help themselves." This was a maxim which covered every situation.

It covered his need now, when he was bewildered and frightened about the future. Feeling himself grow calmer, he realized that he could probably find a school without a teacher in some village in war-torn New England. College graduates did not usually teach in the dirty one-room schools for village children, but he must pocket his pride and do it. The sooner he began looking for a school the better.

Where was he known? Where had he been?

The next day he rode into Hartford, and began making inquiries of people he knew there. Within a few days he was engaged to teach the village school at Glastonbury, Connecticut, where his class from Yale had lodged the summer before.

CHAPTER TWELVE

Schoolmaster Webster

THE BOYS AND girls of Glastonbury were full of excitement one morning a few weeks later. A new schoolmaster had taken over the village school—a very young schoolmaster, people said, with fresh cheeks and boyish, wavy hair. But a very dignified schoolmaster, too, a graduate of Yale College, who knew everything backward and talked in Latin as easily as he did in English.

The woman with whom he lodged had tales to tell as well. How he asked particularly not to have fried pork for breakfast; a piece of cornbread, baked in the ashes of the kitchen fire, would do him nicely. For supper he preferred "a dish of tea" and bread and butter to heartier fare. In his bedroom he wanted chiefly a good table at which to work. A cot would do to sleep on. He would burn plenty of candles, because he meant to study law by himself at night after his day's teaching was done. A schoolmaster like this had never before been seen in Glastonbury, or any other village thereabout.

Trudging down the dusty lanes to school the first morning the children talked eagerly about him. Few of

One of the little girls had brought a red apple for him.

them had waited for the schoolbell to ring, before leaving home. When they reached the one-room building beside the church, they went in hastily, the girls by one door, the boys by another. Hanging their wraps in the vestibule, they entered the room where the new teacher was waiting.

Young Mr. Webster greeted them politely, more politely than any teacher they had ever had. As they took their seats on the long benches, they saw that he had already arranged his desk neatly for work. A bottle of ink and a quill pen in the middle, two or three books on one side, a ruler on the other.

One of the little girls had brought a red apple for him as a token of welcome. This was usually the signal for some giggling and subdued laughter. The new teacher took the apple gravely, thanked the little girl, and turned to arrange a calendar he had pinned upon the wall behind him. Something about his back seemed to suggest that there really was not much need for giggling. Instead of laughing their usual hearty guffaws, the bigger boys shuffled their feet and waited.

In a few minutes, when everyone was in his place, the new teacher rapped on his desk for order.

"Boys and girls," he said. "America is a fine country, engaged now in a great struggle to preserve her liberty. We can help most in that struggle by doing the tasks set before us here. I expect each of you to love his school, to mind his book, and to strive to learn. . . . I will now take the first class in reading."

Somehow after that there was nothing to do but settle down to work.

The work prospered as the winter went on, but young Mr. Webster was not happy in it. It was not that the children did not work faithfully for him; class followed class uninterruptedly through the long day. But the lack of books and writing materials fretted the new teacher. Fifty children and only one spelling book! The New Testament, as a reader, going down a long line of restless, grubby hands!

What kind of education was this to offer the young citizens of a new Republic?

True, the war was still going on; things everywhere were disorganized and unsettled. All the more reason then to make the schools temples of learning and order.

Shivering in the bleak building, young Mr. Webster wondered indignantly why there could not be a better place in which the children could learn their lessons. Watching the big boys try to fold their long legs under low tables, he wondered why all the benches and tables were the same size when the children obviously were not. Trying to explain the countries of Europe, he longed for a map, which would show those countries properly. Hearing class after class recite its lessons in a loud chorus until his ears ached, he wondered how any teacher could be expected to teach half a hundred children in one room. Trying to live and buy his clothes and some law books on a salary of five or six dollars a month, he wondered why teachers were paid barely enough to live on.

Apparently, however, these were questions which no-one had thought to ask before.

At night in his room the hopelessness of the situation tormented him. Bravely, however, he swallowed his discouragement. If he could get through the next two or three years somehow, he could complete his law work, and put schoolroom misery behind him.

Fortunately, the following winter he was able to transfer his teaching to his own village of West Hartford. Here at least he could live at home in his mother's cheerful presence. To Mrs. Webster this hard-working sober young teacher was just her own dear Noah, the son who must be coaxed and pampered a little about his eating.

"Sakes alive, you cannot *eat* your book as well as read it!" she complained, when he brought a book to the supper table.

"After the uproar at school today, 'tis a pleasure to read quietly at supper," answered Noah.

"And your father and me, do we not get one word from so learned a gentleman?"

Noah closed his book. "I'm sorry, Ma, I didn't think. But I have nothing at all to tell you."

"Indeed. A word about my dumplings would not come

amiss. Or some hint to your father as to how the war is going. He gets no time to read the paper."

"I'll help with the milking after supper. I'd like to do more, but I have no time."

"Let the boy be, Mercy," said Mr. Webster. "He is pale and sick already from the double load of teaching and study."

"And what am I trying to do, if not to lift the yoke off his neck for a few moments?" cried Mrs. Webster. "He that used to be so lively! He carries a face now like a parson!"

"A parson I'll never be," said Noah. "But someday, God willing, I'll be something beside a country schoolmaster."

"Of course you will, Son," answered his mother. "From the paper you cover with writing in your room at night, I'd say you mean to be a writer."

"There is so much that is wrong with our schools today," answered Noah. "I have been writing some essays on education. A new nation has been formed on the American continent, and our schools are backward and neglected. There must be some way to improve them."

"If there is, Noah, I'm sure you'll find it. A slight lad, but determined, you always were. Time has not changed you a particle."

"Nor will it," answered Noah firmly. "In this matter I shall not alter."

That winter of the year 1779-80 was a long and cruel one. The snow, which always fell heavily, fell more heavily than usual. When Noah tramped the four miles to school each morning, it lay over all the fences.

The long, cold walk did not make his task of opening the school any easier. On arriving, he had to make a fire in the fireplace as quickly as possible, in order to warm the building a little before the children came. Then the loud clamor of the bell summoned the children to him.

Sometimes the room was so cold that they could barely hold their pens in their fingers. Coming in with wet feet, they sat shivering and sniffling through the long session. Noah Webster did his best for them, but often he felt frustrated and angry. The schools, he knew, were required by law, but the parents of the pupils paid for them. Five shilling each from perhaps fifty parents provided only sixty or seventy dollars a year to pay the teacher. There was no money at all for books or equipment.

On a cold day Noah often felt a little as General Washington must have felt two winters before trying to rally his freezing troops at Valley Forge. Thank God, the war was not going so badly now, although it was not won either. At least, however, the enemy had been driven further south, where it was warmer for the soldiers in winter.

His own war, Noah felt, the war to make a place for himself in a cold and dreary world, was not going well

[93]

at all. The snow, which lay over all the fences when he walked to school in the morning, reminded him of his buried hopes—his great wish to become a lawyer.

The following summer, however, hope revived a little. After writing a good many letters, he secured a small legal position in Litchfield, Connecticut, helping the Recorder of Deeds there with his legal papers. This work he did in the daytime. Night found him, as usual, buried deep in the law books he had been studying ever since he left Yale.

This work persisted through the winter. A dusty law office was not very exciting, but it was vastly better than a country schoolroom. The Recorder, Jedidiah Strong, had a good stove in his office. Around this stove gathered a number of educated men. And if Noah Webster, at twenty-two, talked a good deal more than he should have in these gatherings of older men, it was only what might have been expected. The young schoolmaster had been starving for two years for some place where he could air his views on many subjects!

One subject, which the men talked about a good deal in Judge Strong's office, was the small amount of legal business to be divided among a large number of lawyers in Connecticut. To Noah, of course, this was distressing news. After all, what good was it to become a lawyer, if a man could not hope to get many cases? Other men might live on small earnings, doing the work which they liked best. He had hanging over his head like a sword the debt of six hundred dollars which he owed his father.

Ignoring his anxiety about this as best he could, he kept on with his studies. And in April, 1781, he had the satisfaction of passing his bar examinations in Hartford.

Being now a full-fledged lawyer, he was entitled to sign his name Noah Webster, Esquire, instead of plain Noah Webster. His mother, who cleaned his room at home, found a good many scraps of paper in odd corners, containing nothing but his signature.

"Bless me," she cried, "That's the third paper I've found today, which has nothing on it but 'Noah Webster, Esquire.' Can the boy be daft?"

But the young man who wrote the signature in a fine flourishing hand knew that he was still a long way from becoming the man he longed to be.

CHAPTER THIRTEEN

The School That Failed

APRIL AGAIN, AND once more Noah Webster sat in a small bedroom in his father's house, cudgeling his brains for some means of earning his living. How mad he had been to suppose that he might practise law. With the country upset as it was there was little business for any lawyer. A young man of twenty-two, with no reputation, office or law-books, might sit for a year waiting for a single case.

Sitting idly at home was no part of Noah Webster's plan. He must go forth instantly to "tackle" something. But when he reviewed the kinds of work for which he was fitted, he could not escape the fact that he knew more about teaching than anything else.

All right, if he must teach school, he would teach a good one. No more choruses of dirty children in a cold, bare room. He would open his own school in Sharon, Connecticut, where there were educated families. The school would be held in comfortable quarters, with proper books and equipment. The pupils would pay twenty-six dollars a year for instruction in "Reading, Writing, Arithmetic, the English Language, Latin, Greek, and Vocal Music." "Ladies" would be encouraged to come as well as "Gentlemen." "P.S. If any persons are desirous of acquainting themselves with the French language, they may be under the instruction of an accomplished master." So ran the advertisement which he ran in the *Connecticut Courant* in June.

Reading this program for his school today, it is easy to laugh at young Mr. Webster. Not yet twenty-three years old, he looked and acted as solemn as an owl in his black coat and white neckcloth. A farmer's son still, he hoped to establish a select academy for young "ladies and gentlemen."

The pupils, who came to the spacious attic of John Cotton Smith's house in Sharon on July 1st, when the school opened, were distinctly above Noah Webster socially. Three daughters of a Mr. Livingston, who had fled from New York City to escape the War. Two of the Livingston cousins. Frederick and Barton Prevost, also of New York. Children of other prominent families, too. A full baker's dozen of young "ladies and gentlemen," who expected superior instruction from an "accomplished master."

And what did they do to this ardent young teacher? They laughed at him. The girls thought he was stiff and dull beyond words. Young Miss Juliana Smith, sister of the man in whose house the school was held, tittered behind her fan during the singing classes which she attended.

[97]

"He reminds me of a horse with his long face!" she whispered to her neighbor.

Mr. Webster gave out the name of the song they were to sing, and sounded the pitch.

"Why does he always fold his hands behind his back like a little general?" whispered Miss Smith's neighbor.

"They are nice, firm hands, too," answered Miss Smith. "Do you suppose he does that because he is nervous?"

"Probably. Fancy setting yourself up as a teacher, and then being so nervous your hands tremble. They say he is nobody but a farmer's son, who went to Yale College."

"His conversation is as dull as ditch-water. But Papa says he works hard, and is bound to get somewhere."

"So does a horse!" said the neighbor unkindly. "Only a horse can't talk. This man talks and talks about everything."

"He thinks all the other schools in the country are terrible. He says they need books and maps and bigger desks and everything."

"So that a lot of dirty children can learn things they don't need to know, I suppose."

"I presume so."

"Ladies, ladies!" rapped Mr. Webster. "Please pay attention to the singing!"

The young ladies straightened their faces. But they were not impressed by this new teacher in the badly-tied neckcloth. The fact that he was tired to death from days of teaching and nights of study, carried on over a period of years, did not occur to them at all.

In his heart Noah Webster knew that the young ladies of Sharon did not like him. This offended him deeply. The parents of his pupils, he knew, were well pleased with his teaching. Then why did the young ladies at the singing classes laugh at him behind their fans?

The next thought which he had was more typical of a Connecticut Yankee. Why should he waste his time teaching a lot of silly, rich girls to spout French and English poetry!

What a fool he had been to come over to Sharon to start a school of this sort. The new United States needed schools, but not like this one. Only last week, on the 28th of September, the British General Cornwallis had surrendered to General Washington at Yorktown, Virginia. Soon the men who had fought six and a half years for American independence would come straggling home to New England.

Ragged and worn, they would find their farms going to pieces without them. Ignorant though many of them were, they would send their children hopefully to the village schools for a little "learning." These were the boys and girls he would like to help. These were the schools which must be made truly "American."

He did not intend to go back to teaching a singsong school beside a church in some obscure village. The time for that had gone by. But he would begin to write some kind of decent textbooks for these village schools. A whole series of schoolbooks, containing everything the boys and girls of America needed to know!

And so it was that on October 9, 1781, Noah Webster closed his school at Sha on only three months after it opened. A determined young teacher in a deserted attic packed his belongings once more.

CHAPTER FOURTEEN

The Blue-Backed Speller

ALL THROUGH THE following winter Noah Webster tried to find some kind of legal work or business position, which would support him. In this he was unsuccessful.

The havoc, which followed the long war, was appalling. The Colonies had lost nearly everything but liberty in the struggle. Homes had been burned over wide areas; the farms had gone to seed; many of the cattle had been destroyed; the foreign trade, on which the farmers depended for a little money, was gone.

There was no adequate local government for the separate States; money had been printed by the Continental Congress, by the separate States, by private banks. People looked with suspicion on these pieces of paper, which said $2., $5., or $10. on them, but which might not buy a quarter's worth of anything. A sack of cornmeal or a string of home-grown tobacco was more valuable.

Farther south, Noah heard, conditions were not so bad. There the rich plantations had not been molested. A little trade with the West Indies in cotton and tobacco was still possible. The problem of stony fields and bad weather had never bothered the southern planters as it had the farmers of New England. The New England men were hard as flint and stubborn, too, because of the battles they had fought with their own stubborn fields. Some of this flint was in Noah Webster. He would pack up and ride south, carrying his ideals with him.

Tying his manuscripts in a large bundle, he set out in May, 1782, for richer pastures. Fifty miles in a rocking stagecoach brought him to the Hudson River at Newburgh. Crossing there, he traveled another twenty miles to the town of Goshen, New York. But farther than this he could not go. He had now only seventy-five cents in his pocket, and not very good clothes on his back. He must get some kind of job at once. He found one in the local high school at Goshen, where he would teach for ten dollars a month in silver money.

During the next few months in Goshen, Noah gathered his whirling wits about him. He had been tossed about so much during the last four years that he could not always think clearly. His health had suffered, too. He could not sleep well or enjoy his meals.

Sometimes a sense of failure sat like a raven on his table. He had tried to become a lawyer, and failed. He had tried to open his own school and failed. He had tried to secure a business position and failed.

But then he would turn to the manuscript on which he wrote faithfully every night until long after midnight.

People looked with suspicion on these pieces of paper.

The American Instructor, he called it. It was the first book in his series of textbooks, a simple speller fundamentally but also a ripe plum of patriotism and courage.

Into writing this textbook he put his whole soul night after night. Already his mind leaped ahead from the simple words he put on paper to more and more glorious books, which would follow. The daily task, however, consisted in progressing logically from simple syllables like *ba, be, bi, bo* and *bu,* suitable for children in pinafores, to a list of towns in the United States and a table of important dates in American history. No kings and queens and counties of England here. Nor any long descriptions of the Devil and his ways! The earlier spelling-books contained plenty of both.

In August, while the book was still green and unfinished, he carried it to Philadelphia, Princeton, New York and New Haven for criticism by college professors. The men to whom he showed the book were a little bewildered by his visits. Who was this unknown young teacher of twenty-four, bringing a spelling-book to college professors? What did it matter how children learned to spell? What did it have to do with college work?

Patiently, and not too modestly, Webster explained that the beginning of education was important, too. What a barefoot boy learned in a village school influenced his whole life.

"As the twig is bent, so is the tree inclined," he quoted to them.

He had other queer ideas about schooling, too, ideas which everyone accepts today as a matter of course, but which in 1782 were new and startling.

"The children should have nothing to discourage them," he said earnestly. "A simple reward on quarter-day is far better than a dozen beatings."

"Oh, there you are wrong, Mr. Webster," the older teachers declared. "You remember the old saying, 'Spare the rod and spoil the child.'"

"An old saying, but a false one!" cried Mr. Webster. "Who can work well with the fear of a strap hanging over him?"

The graybeards shook their heads, unconvinced. Teachers always had strapped pupils, who did not learn quickly. It must be the right way.

"And what does it matter how farmers pronounce their words?" they asked, noting that in his introduction he begged for better pronunciation.

"Some farm boys in this country cannot even read and write!" cried Mr. Webster. "How can they be good Americans, when they are so ignorant?"

"Well, perhaps you are right," agreed the professors. "To tell the truth, we probably have never thought much about it."

In New Haven, President Stiles listened to his words more attentively. After all Noah was a former Yale boy —one of the most brilliant students the college had graduated. But Dr. Stiles did not like the name of his

"Nonsense!" exclaimed Mr. Webster. "Who can work well with the fear of the strap over him!"

book. He persuaded him to give it a more resounding title.

A GRAMMATICAL INSTITUTE
OF THE
ENGLISH LANGUAGE
Comprising
An easy, concise, & systematic Method
of Education, designed for the Use of
English Schools in America,

he called it. Fortunately, this clumsy title only lasted through the first two or three editions of the book. Later editions were called *The American Spelling Book.* In any case, no-one ever spoke of the book after it was published as anything but Webster's Spelling Book.

This Spelling Book, which Noah finally completed in January, 1783, was a little volume of 119 pages packed so full of good things that it almost burst its blue cover. History, geography, science, the Creation of the World, How to be a Good Boy, the rivers of North America, the tribes of Africa, the spelling of proper names, the towns and counties of the different States, everything anyone could think of was in that so-called Spelling Book. With a book like that in his hands a schoolboy could learn something every day in the year.

The order in which he learned it was comfortably progressive. Beginning with *ba, be, bi, bo, bu* in Table I, the young student went on in Table II to words of three and four letters like *bag, beg, big, bog* and *bug.* Then came some easy reading lessons, using these words.

The first reading lesson went as follows:

Be a good child; mind your book; love your school, and strive to learn.

Tell no tales; call no ill names; you must not lie, nor swear, nor cheat, nor steal.

Play not with bad boys, use no ill words at play; spend your time well; live in peace, and shun all strife. This is the way to make good men love you, and save your soul from pain and woe.

This was lesson 12. But in case it did not sink in, here is lesson 13:

A good child will not lie, swear nor steal. He will be good at home, and ask to read his book; when he gets up, he will wash his hands and face clean; he will comb his hair, and make haste to school; he will not play by the way as bad boys do.

Lessons 14 and 15 were about—how to be a good boy! After that the Speller talked about other things.

Table XIV went on to harder words—*apron, barefoot, rhubarb, bracelet, parcel* and *parlour.*

Table XV contained some of the proverbs and maxims which all the world of those days quoted on every possible occasion.

> Hope well and have well.
>
> Two eyes see more than one.
>
> A burnt child dreads the fire.
>
> The new broom sweeps clean.

By Table XVII, the young student was getting on to really splendid words like *lubricate, nightingale, rheumatism, bayonet* and *poignancy*. After a few more proverbs he arrived at *combustion, digestion, multiplication* and *glorification.*

And now having perspired his way through a good deal of hard learning, the young reader reached his reward. The middle of the book was given over to a series of quaint fables. *The Boy Who Stole the Apples, The Country Maid and Her Milk-Pail, The Fox and the Swallow, The Cat and the Old Rat, The Bear and the Two Friends.*

The Boy Who Stole the Apples went as follows:

An old Man found a rude Boy upon one of the Trees stealing Apples, and desired him to come down; but the young Sauce-box told him plainly he would not.

Won't you, said the old Man, then I will fetch you down; so he pulled up some Tufts of Grass, and threw at him; but this only made the Youngster laugh, to think the old Man should pretend to beat him out of the Tree with Grass only.

Well, well, said the old Man, if neither Words nor Grass will do, I must try what Virtue there is in Stones; so the old Man pelted him heartily with Stones, which soon made the young Chap hasten down from the Tree, and beg the old Man's Pardon.

MORAL

If good Words and gentle Means will not reclaim the Wicked, they must be dealt with in a more severe Manner.

FABLE **I.** *Of the Boy that stole Apples.*

A page from "Webster's Spelling Book."

Table XV told the *History of the Creation of the World* in the following quaint words:

In six days God made the world, and all things that are

in it. He made the sun to shine by day, and the moon to give light by night. He made all the beasts that walk on the earth, all the birds that fly in the air, and all the fish that swim in the sea. Each herb, and plant, and tree, is the work of his hands. All things, both great and small, that live, and move, and breathe in this wide world, to him do owe their birth, to him their life. And God saw that all the things he had made were good. But as yet there was not a man to till the ground: so God made man of the dust of the earth, and gave him rule over all that he had made. And the man gave names to all the beasts of the field; the fowls of the air, and the fish of the sea. But there was not found a helpmeet for man; so God brought on him a deep sleep, and then took from his side a rib, of which he made a wife, and gave her to the man, and her name was Eve: And from these two came all the sons of man.

Table XLII was by way of review. It contained *The Description of a Good Boy* and *The Description of a Bad Boy!*

Table XLVI was a tough nut to crack. The spelling of proper names, including *Abraham, Beelzebub, Gabriel, Janizary, Sadducee* and *Dionyssius.* Also rivers, tribes, towns and mountains such as *Eskimaux, Catawba, Appalachian* and *Ticonderoga.*

So much for the body of the speller, which was to be meat and drink for farm boys and girls all over the land. The introduction and footnotes were useful, too.

In the introduction young Mr. Webster pleaded for an "American" language. Bravely he insisted that good

Yankee words like *whittle* and *chore* be given the dignity which they deserved.

The footnotes, however, begged the boys and girls to pronounce their words more carefully than they sometimes did.

Say *ask,* not *ax,* he urged; *chimney,* not *chimbly; negro,* not *neger; spirit,* not *sperit; soldier* for *sojer; Indian* for *Injun, getting* for *gittin'.*

"I have written this book," he said sadly, "to correct an atrocious pronunciation which exists everywhere."

An ear, tuned to language, can be a painful appendage. Noah Webster was often in places where men pronounced their words distinctly out of tune. However, he did not intend to let this situation go unheeded. *It Is Hard to Teach an Old Dog New Tricks,* he wrote sadly, thinking of the older generation of readers. But *As the Twig Is Bent So the Tree Is Inclined.* This meant the new generation—the children all over the land, who would come to his Speller for information.

The first edition of Webster's Speller did not contain quite all of the material mentioned here. But second and third editions were more inclusive.

It was with a sigh of satisfaction that Webster wrote the last page of his Speller in January, 1783.

CHAPTER FIFTEEN

The Speller Makes Friends

THE NEXT PROBLEM which young Mr. Webster had to face, after he finished writing his Speller, was to get his book published. Authors always have this problem. In Noah Webster's case, however, the problem was many times more difficult that it would be today.

The first thing he discovered, on returning to Hartford from Goshen, was that books had never been published in America. There simply were no American books.

The next thing he learned was that there were no copyright laws in the various States, which would protect a young author from having his book copied and sold without payment of royalties.

The next thing he learned was that there were almost no bookstores, where the book might be offered for sale. Possibly a drug store or two in the towns would undertake to sell a few copies. In the villages it would have to be offered, if offered at all, in the general store where people bought coffee and sugar and molasses, as well as clothing and sticks of peppermint candy.

Any other writer but Mr. Webster might have been overcome by these discouraging prospects. But by the age of twenty-four Noah had a fine grip on the maxim that had seen him through heavy difficulties before. *God Helps Those Who Help Themselves.*

Without even waiting to find a publisher, he set out by stagecoach to visit some of the principal cities in the thirteen States, where the State Legislatures were meeting. Armed with letters of introduction, and a willingness to talk about his forthcoming book, he succeeded in getting copyright laws passed in six States before Christmas—Connecticut, Massachusetts, Maryland, New Jersey, New Hampshire and Rhode Island. In town after town, too, he called on the local schoolmasters and preachers, urging them to promote the sale of an *American* textbook for *American* children.

And now to get the book published. In New York, Boston, Philadelphia, where was a man willing to print 5,000 copies of his little work without being paid for it in advance? There was no such man in any of these cities. As a poor schoolmaster, of course, Noah could not possibly pay the costs of printing the book.

Returning to Hartford, he called on Barzillai Hudson and George Goodwin, publishers of the *Connecticut Courant,* which he had read since he was a child. In the grimy newspaper office an arrangement was made by which they would print 5,000 copies of the Speller and wait a little for their money. If the Speller did not sell, however, Noah would be liable for the full cost of the printing. As a poor schoolmaster, already heavily in debt to his father, he could hardly hope to pay off these costs in a lifetime of frugal living.

The little book made its appearance in October in the blue cloth cover, which it wore forever after. Costing one shilling and twopence a copy, or about thirty cents, it began to appear on store counters along with the calico and cheese. In the drug stores it lay beside hair-oil or tonic, innocently offering its Method of Education to people who came in looking distractedly for medicine.

"Eh, eh, what is this?" inquired a weathered farmer, who came looking for something to soothe an ailing child. "A new spelling-book! What's the matter with the old Dilworth out of which I learned my letters?"

"The man who wrote this book claims it is an *American* Speller. He says Dilworth is old-fashioned."

"Old-fashioned, eh? Why, my father before me learned out of Dilworth!"

"Yes? Well, times have changed, it seems. Some of these newfangled ideas are purty good."

"Hmm. Well, p'raps Josiah (or Mirandy or Ebenezer) might get some good out've it. What did ye say it cost?"

"Only one shilling and tuppence. I'll let ye have one for a quarter."

"All right, I'll take it. That is, if ye're sure it's not un-religious. I don't want no story-books coming into my house."

"No, no. It's quite respectable. And a sight more cheerful than the old Dilworth speller."

"Well, well. Ma'll be that surprised when I come home with a new spelling-book. She sent me in for medicine. Guess I'd better be gittin' along with it."

"Here ye are then. And I hope the shaver is soon better."

"I expect he will be. Funny thing about Ma. She don't hold with dipping a sick child. When I was young, it was into the tub head-foremost for most any kind of sickness."

"Well, this medicine'll help a lot. I've taken it myself to break a fever."

"Ye hev, eh? Well, thanks, again."

And out the farmer went with his newfangled medicine and newfangled speller, prepared to be modern at any cost.

The boys and girls in the reopened schools took to Webster's Spelling Book instantly. They liked the fables, which came as a reward for learning new words. They liked the pictures, too, which appeared in later editions: Mr. Webster himself with his hair standing up like porcupine quills; the fox and the bear and the milk-maid illustrating the fables.

Not only children, but grown people liked the little book. Farmers and judges and statesmen, teachers and preachers gave it their approval. During the first nine months after it was published, the first edition of 5,000

Frontiersmen, laboring over letters in far wildernesses,
spelled their words as Mr. Webster recommended.

copies sold rapidly. Subsequent editions sold well, and were even larger.

In the course of the next ten years probably a million copies sold throughout the United States. As peace came to the country, and more and more schools were opened, the demand for the book increased steadily. The Speller went west in covered wagons, crossed rivers and mountains, stood on a special shelf with the Bible and almanack in country homes, and became the backbone of American education. In the course of Noah Webster's lifetime nearly 25,000,000 copies were sold. After he died it continued to sell up to a total of 100,000,000 copies. Probably no book, excepting the Bible, has had a better sale over a period of years.

The effect of all this popularity was, of course, far-reaching. Since people everywhere read and studied the Speller, they pronounced their words largely as it did. *Ask* did replace *ax* in people's mouths. Men blushed and muttered again, when they accidentally said *chimbly* for *chimney.* In writing letters, too, under frontier conditions, they spelled their words as Mr. Webster recommended. By candlelight and smoky lamps, working with a goose quill pen on smudgy paper, they wrote the family back home in Kentucky or Massachusetts or Pennsylvania, according to Mr. Webster.

And what of young Noah Webster, who passed his twenty-fifth birthday a few weeks after the first edition of the Speller was published? He returned quietly from his copyright journeys, rented a room in Hartford, and settled down to look for legal business. He also slept better at night, knowing that a little money would now be coming in from another source than legal practice.

The Speller sold for thirty cents a copy. On the first 5,000 copies Noah received one hundred and thirty-six dollars. To a young man, who still owed his father six hundred dollars for his education, this was not a rich profit. But to a young man who had risked a lifetime of debt to publish the book at all, and who had taught school for months at a time at five or six dollars a month, it was a good beginning.

More satisfying, also, than the money itself was the feeling that he had done what he set out to do. America needed an American schoolbook, and he had given it to her. It was the first of a long list of patriotic services, which he was to render his beloved country.

CHAPTER SIXTEEN

More Books and a Pamphlet

IN HIS ROOM in Hartford Noah was able to live the kind of life he loved. Plenty of cheap paper and pens. A shelf of books for reference. Without quite realizing it, this fiery young man had millions of words in him, which he wanted to put on paper.

Behind the words, of course, were the ideas which prompted them. Probably no man living at that time had more exact opinions on more subjects than he did. His busy brain worked night and day classifying, rejecting and accepting various opinions.

The first writing he did was the second volume of his *Grammatical Institute,* this time a Grammar, which would explain how to put words and sentences together correctly. The first part of the Grammar was correct and formal—it asked and answered its own questions in orderly fashion.

What is Grammar?
Explain the Noun.
How many Genders are there?
What is a Verb?
What is a Sentence?

Young readers today still plow through a discussion of these points until they know the answers.

The second part of the Grammar, however, plunged into horrible examples of how *not* to talk and write. With each day's lesson came a fresh crop of faulty phrases and sentences for the student to make right. This, for example:

> Philadelphia are a large city, it stand on the west side of the river Delaware, and am the most regular city in America. . . . I were much delighted with it; I wishes that you could see it.

Again quite frankly he wrote:

> The boy's who I admire are those that study.

By the time he reached the sixth lesson, he swung into fable-form, making his little story a hash of misconstruction for the young reader to correct as he read. Reading about a fierce mother goose, his readers were asked to recast the following:

Sixth Lesson

Once upon a time a goose feed its young by a pond side; and a goose, in such circumstances, be always proud and punctilious. If any other animal, without the least design offend, happen pass that way, the goose be immediately at it. The pond, she say, be hers, and she maintain her right in it and support her honor, while she have a bill hiss, or a wing flutter. In this manner she drive away ducks, pigs and chickens; nay even the insidious cat be seen to scamper.

This Grammar, published separately in March, 1784, was combined in later editions with the Speller, so that the two were published in one volume. The later editions also used illustrations more freely—the dim, crooked woodcuts, which the printers of that day hacked out by hand. The blue cloth cover on this combined Speller never changed. The sight of it on a shelf in a country store became as familiar as the bolts of calico or jars of peppermint candy, which stood side by side.

In the educational field now, there remained only for Webster to write the Reader that would complete his series. This was a comparatively easy task. Obviously it should contain as much American material as possible. Indeed nowadays we would call it a geography or history of the United States, since it contained a great deal of both.

The Contents shows how faithfully Noah Webster stuck to his theory that an American Reader should contain information about America. The book included the following:

The Way to Wealth
    By Benjamin Franklin
History of Columbus
Discovery and Settlement of North America
Geography of the United States

Brief History of the late War
Address of Congress to the People of Great Britain
Declaration of Independence

This Reader, then, was to replace the thumbed copies of the New Testament or Psalms, which had been used as readers in the schools up to 1785. Boys and girls struggling through the big words in the Bible, must have welcomed this change. It is to be hoped, too, that in using the new lesson-book, the teachers remembered Webster's solemn declaration that "sparing the rod" did *not* "spoil the child." On the contrary, he insisted, children learned more when they were not constantly expecting a blow from a birch rod for their errors.

If he had been a little less patriotic than he was, or if the times had been different, Webster would have realized when he compiled his Reader that it left out many things. Fine examples of English prose, for instance, the history of *other* countries besides the United States, any glimpses of scientific facts. But for boys and girls concerned chiefly with gathering a little Reading, Writing and Arithmetic between summers of heavy work on the farms, his Reader was obviously the right diet.

It was a lonely life which Noah led in Hartford during those years, but he liked it. Ideas flowed luxuriously, no matter in what direction he turned his mind. Few clients drifted in for legal advice, but he was happy with his writing.

Sometimes on a Sunday he went out to the old home

in West Hartford to visit his mother. It was nice to see her, but he was glad to be away from the farm now. In many ways he had outgrown it. He did not know quite what to say to his father; the nieces and nephews who filled the house to overflowing on family holidays made conversation impossible.

Shrewdly his mother guessed the source of his restlessness.

"There now, I know you want to *talk,* and there isn't anyone here who can talk with you."

"It's fine to see you, Ma, and the orchard and the meadows."

"Yes, but I know *you.* You'd rather have your nose poked in a book, and a plate of raisins beside you, than all the Sunday dinners in Christendom."

"I've been writing some newspaper articles. There's so many things needed here in Connecticut."

"And all over the country, too, I've no doubt. Surely you can find something to say about the way our *nation* is being run?"

"Well, as a matter of fact, I have," confessed Noah a little shamefacedly. Who but his mother could admire him whole-heartedly, and yet make him feel that he must not take himself too seriously?

"Tell me about the newspaper articles," urged his mother.

"We need better *national* government in this country," cried Noah. "I've been writing about that."

"You mean the State government does not work properly?"

"It isn't that, Ma. But there is no central government at all. Questions of money, mail service, the army, navigation, and taxes are always coming up. The Articles of Confederation, adopted three years ago, are not enough. We need a central government to hold us together. The Union will fall apart without it."

"That would be a sad thing after six and a half years of war, wouldn't it?"

"Exactly. Our statesmen are worried about it. General Washington, Benjamin Franklin, and Alexander Hamilton have expressed their fears."

"And Mr. Noah Webster, too?"

"Well, to tell the truth I *have* been writing a pamphlet. It is called *Sketches of American Policy.*"

"And what do you intend to do with this pamphlet?"

"I shall have it published, and take it to various people."

"Oh, you are going on a trip then? Have you plenty of clean shirts to take with you?"

"Ma, what would I do without you? Our country needs a new Constitution, and you ask me if I have plenty of clean shirts!"

"That is a woman's duty," answered Mrs. Webster with dignity. "And an important one, too."

CHAPTER SEVENTEEN

The Open Road

DURING THE NEXT two years Noah Webster might well be described as the Man on Horseback. Paul Revere rode feverishly over the countryside one night, to rouse the farmers to protect their country. Noah Webster rode for weeks at a time, rousing the people of the United States to their duty as Americans.

His first journey was to the southern states. Sending on a box of books from Hartford, he set out one morning in May, 1785, to distribute his little pamphlet and his schoolbooks to important men in most of the American cities. A determined figure in neat black clothes, he took his seat expectantly in the mud-splashed coach that would go first to New York, then to Philadelphia, and from there—in two long days of travel—the hundred miles to Baltimore.

As he rode along in the coach hour after hour, he had a chance to think of many things. One of them was that he was tired of New England—that rocky country of stubborn men, some of them blind to the need for stronger national government. His articles in the papers had brought down a good deal of abuse on his head.

"The dignity, safety, and happiness of America," he would write, "are inseparably connected with a union of all the States."

In return his opponents would write of him that he was "a sneaky, snaky, faint-hearted Whig," whose "dirty squibs will avail . . . no more than spitting against the north wind." Sometimes in his room at night, he wondered why he worked so hard for the good of the country, when so many men opposed him. Then there would glow in his heart the feeling that his country needed him to work night and day for greater unity. The fact that he was in the stagecoach now, with a quantity of his precious pamphlets and books going on ahead, made him very happy.

Ten days later he was in Baltimore. The city was a great surprise to him. A sprawling, dirty, bustling town, full of sailors and Negroes and newly-arrived immigrants with their bundles from overseas. He did not know quite what to think. The ships in the harbor dominated everything. The buildings were set all higgledy-piggledy in crowded streets. There were more stores and taverns and warehouses than he had seen anywhere before. It was his first visit to a sea-port.

Taking a firm grip on himself, he called on ministers and teachers and judges, telling them about his schoolbooks and his pamphlet urging a strong, national government. To the merchants of Baltimore he carried copies of his Speller and Reader. To the legislature he carried a plea for copyright laws in Maryland. Only a man of great energy could have accomplished so much in so little time.

From Baltimore he set forth on horseback for Alexandria, Virginia, riding the muddy roads in his second-best suit, with his Sunday best in the saddle-bags behind him. The roads were simply dreadful—rough highways, paved with planks, where they were paved at all. The ditches on either side were sometimes ten feet deep. But to jog along on horsback was better than riding in the swaying coach with its slow progress of sometimes only three or four miles an hour.

The Man on Horseback was happy indeed.

From Alexandria, Virginia, young Mr. Webster set out on the morning of May 19 for Mt. Vernon. Carrying with him a letter of introduction, he planned to call on General Washington himself.

The General's home at Mt. Vernon was, of course, different from anything he had known. General Washington owned 70,000 acres of land in Virginia and 40,000 acres in a nearby State. He had over 300 Negroes to farm his estate. In his stables were dozens of fine horses—to the day of his death he enjoyed hunting, fishing, and riding over his fields and woodlands.

The house itself, where Noah Webster called, was more impressive than any home he had ever seen. Its wide verandahs, spacious parlors and host of Negro servants suggested a leisure and ease which were not possible in New England. The ladies in their pretty dresses were unlike any ladies he had known. His heart warmed to them.

Would he stay overnight? Yes, he would be delighted.

Did he like fried chicken and gravy for dinner? That would be very nice.

Would he join the ladies around the piano? Well, in New England villages the ladies did not sing and play the piano after supper, but Noah Webster had himself done a good deal of singing while he was in college. He would be happy to join the ladies in the brilliantly-lighted parlors where dozens of candles blazed in crystal chandeliers.

Noah Webster would never be a part of any life of this kind; he was too much the stern scholar for that. But this night—for a few hours—he enjoyed the life of a Virginia mansion. How glad he was that the ruffle of his best white shirt had not become rumpled in the saddle-bags.

The one thing which he refused at dinner was a serving of molasses with his rice and cornbread.

"We have enough of that in my country," he said. "In our porridge, over the pudding, with baked apples, dumplings, everything!"

Later, in the General's library, he and his host talked far into the night. General Washington was interested in his schoolbooks; he wanted to hear more about them. He knew, also, that Noah Webster felt that there should be more and better schools throughout the land.

"You are right about that," said the General. "Here in Virginia schools are few and far between. Even among the wealthiest planters, the men and women cannot always write their own names."

This information shocked Noah Webster deeply. How glad he was now that in every New England village there was a drafty schoolhouse beside every church. The country boys, who came plowing through the snow on winter morning in cotton trousers, had always had an opportunity to learn to read and write after a fashion. There was a softness about life in Virginia of which he could not approve. Nevertheless, he enjoyed spending the night with General Washington and his family at Mt. Vernon.

From Mt. Vernon, Webster went back to Baltimore, and from there he set out on a sailing-vessel for Charleston, South Carolina.

What a journey that was! Twenty-seven days on the little vessel, first pounded by wind and rain, then becalmed in glassy waters. The food—never very good at best—became worse and worse. He could not eat the fried salt pork and moldy potatoes which appeared on the table. How he longed for some of his mother's freshly-baked cornbread and buttermilk, or a handful of raisins beside the fire in his room at Hartford.

Charleston itself, of course, was delightful. A sleepy, languorous city, heavy with the smell of magnolias and azaleas. Beautiful old houses with iron balconies. Negroes in clean blue cotton trousers; the women in brightly-colored bandanas. The cries of peddlers in the streets wakened him in the morning.

"Strawbe'ies, fresh strawbe'ies," they droned.

The wild strawberries in the corners of the pasture in Connecticut were not as sweet as these.

But he did not forget his business in Charleston either. Before he left he saw that his Speller and Reader were accepted as the official schoolbooks for South Carolina.

His voyage back to Baltimore was not as lengthy nor as painful as the unfortunate trip down. In eight days the tidy little sloop sailed up the coast and into Baltimore harbor.

Settling down in the city, he gave himself up to active work. Having advertised that he would start a singing-school, he trained ten singers for a concert on September 4. The concert was a great success, bringing in more pupils. For a brief period his school flourished.

The reason why it did not continue was easy to find. Again in Baltimore, as he had in Sharon, he found himself teaching frivolous young ladies, who thought more about their dresses and hair-ornaments than they did

What a journey that was!

about education. For a few weeks he tried to live up to this social atmosphere. In his diary he wrote that he had paid a gold guinea, worth almost ten dollars, for silk stockings to wear with new buckled slippers, which cost two dollars. He also bought a pair of kid gloves to wear to his singing-classes.

His pupils came from good families, and paid handsomely for their instruction. Twenty-one pupils paid a dollar and a half each for books, and a dollar for six weeks' lessons.

Wishing to keep up with the social side of his new situation, Noah gave a dinner for his pupils, at which three dozen bottles of wine were served. And then his natural reaction set in. Looking at himself in his steel mirror the next morning, he realized that he was not the man to go in for this type of entertainment. A plain farmer's son from Connecticut had no business wearing silk stockings that cost a small fortune and buying wine by the dozen bottles.

His pupils should be plain people, the men in the street who talked a careless, corrupt English that left him gasping. They said "neger" for "negro" and "ain't" for "are not" with every breath. Sometimes he could only guess at the meanings of the words they used. Boatloads of immigrants, too, were arriving daily, with their own peculiar pronunciation, even when they came from English-speaking countries.

With his customary abruptness Mr. Webster closed his

singing-school late in August, and began to write a series of lectures on the English language, which would draw attention to mistakes and wrong meanings. More clearly than ever now he saw the need for an American language, with rules of pronunciation which would be the same everywhere. His schoolbooks would accomplish this for the young people. His lectures would do it for men and women, whose school-days were already over.

Everywhere he went he talked so earnestly about these problems that some people were offended. Sometimes they called him "the little monarch." Later on in his life Webster acquired more modesty; at this period of his life he was still something of the raw young man from Connecticut full of his own virtues. Yet what would America have done without him? His courage and insight were invaluable. Let the suave manners and less abrupt approach come later. Where other men lolled in taverns or paid court to the ladies, he toiled hour after hour at his writing-table, striving to serve his country.

Six weeks later his course of five lectures was complete. Putting an advertisement in the paper, he announced that he would talk for five evenings at a dollar per person for each evening on the following subjects: the History of the English Language, Pronunciation, Errors in Pronouncing, Errors in the Use of Words, and General Remarks on Education.

Thirty persons came to the first lecture, more after that.

After completing the course in Baltimore, he passed on to Annapolis, and other Maryland cities. The winter progressed, and so did he. On Valentine's Day, 1786, he reached Philadelphia to lecture at the University of Pennsylvania.

CHAPTER EIGHTEEN

A Busy Traveler

PHILADELPHIA WELCOMED Noah Webster in a way the southern cities had not. The hard-riding young planters of Virginia had not paid much attention to the young schoolmaster in his black clothes, who came riding in to say that America needed better schoolbooks and a stronger national government. At Williamsburg, Virginia, only six persons came to his first lecture. At Petersburg no-one came at all.

But now he was in the snug city beside the Susquehanna. Quakers had settled Philadelphia. Quakers lived in its neat red brick houses.

Philadelphia had provided its share of leaders for the Revolution. The men of the city loved to get together and talk. From warehouses and offices they gathered in the taverns along the waterfront to discuss politics over a plate of fried oysters or good Quaker dishes like scrapple or cheese-cake.

Noah Webster, whose finicky appetite had often rebelled at the fried pork and tasteless boiled dinners of New England, felt much at home among these Quakers. Happily he went about the city, calling on prominent men and making arrangements for his lectures. If he was to succeed at all on his lecture-tour, it would be in a place like this.

One of the men on whom he called was Benjamin Franklin, the grand old man of the Revolution, who had done so much to help America win her independence. Franklin was now eighty years old, and Noah Webster only twenty-seven, but he welcomed the young teacher cordially. Indeed an opportunity to talk was all that Franklin wanted.

"They tell me that you are interested in making a phonetic alphabet with simpler spelling for English words," he said to Noah. "I have been interested in that for a long time. In fact, I have made some notes for it."

Noah studied the notes carefully. *Hav* for *have, eg* for *egg, hed* for *head, bilt* for *built*.

"All silent letters should be omitted, shouldn't they?" he asked Mr. Franklin.

"Of course," answered his host. "And the spelling of a word should indicate exactly how it is pronounced. *Mean* should be spelled *meen, key* as *kee, his* as *hiz, daughter* as *dawter*."

"It would certainly save a great deal of trouble in and out of the schoolroom," agreed Webster. "But it would have to be worked out into a system that was entirely logical and complete."

"That is too much of a task for an old man like me," said Mr. Franklin. "But I think you should undertake it."

"Indeed I would like to," answered Noah Webster. "Of course the most pressing need in America at the moment is for a new system of national government. Have you seen my pamphlet on that subject? It is called *Sketches of American Policy*."

"I haven't seen it, but I will read it with pleasure if you will send me a copy," answered Mr. Franklin. "Our country is in grave danger through its lack of a strong central government. The States are bound to quarrel and clash among themselves without it."

"Exactly," cried Noah Webster. "But many men are against it. I have been ridiculed and contradicted."

"You must learn to expect that," said Mr. Franklin. "No man works for a good cause without a great deal of opposition."

"I know," said Webster. "I have to keep reminding myself to go steadily on in spite of it."

"If you have learned that lesson you are on the road to success," answered Franklin.

The lectures, which began on February 28, were well-received, and profitable. Over a hundred persons came to the first one. This was a great relief to Webster because he was often worried about money. When he was traveling about like this he had many expenses. His board, lodging, and laundry, a horse to ride or a ticket for the stagecoach, advertisements in the newspapers, a hall in which to lecture.

The royalties from his books gave him a small sum to

fall back on. A few weeks of poor attendance at his lectures, however, might use up all his ready money. And yet he could not live in cheap lodgings or eat in back-street restaurants. Whatever the strain of travel, his clothes must be neat and tidy. A torn ruffle on his best shirt meant that he must buy a new one immediately. If he lost a silver buckle from his shoe he must buy a new pair for three or four dollars. Like all young men trying to make their way in the world, Noah Webster had many such secret problems, which he could not mention to anyone.

In Philadelphia, for a few weeks these problems smoothed away. The weather was cold and foggy, a damp wind irritated his throat, but everything else was satisfactory. Small wonder that he strutted a little when he talked about his lectures, or wrote to his publishers:

"I am beginning to make a bustle. The Philadelphians say that my remarks are new and my purpose laudable."

From Philadelphia Webster went to New York City for five weeks, from there to Albany, to Hartford, to New Haven, Springfield, Worcester, Boston, Salem, Portsmouth, Newburyport, Providence, New London and Norwich.

Everywhere he went he heard people complaining about the lack of money.

"I have three sacks of feathers—the finest goose down," said a farmer in a store in Rhode Island, "but no-one has money to buy them. And I need money to pay my taxes."

"I have lambs to sell," said another farmer, "good fat sheep they'll be, but no-one can buy them. If I could get my hands on a little Spanish silver, I'd feel free to let my son get married."

"There's not a shilling to be had anywhere," said another. "My turkeys sell for three shillings, they are fine, fat birds and people want 'em, but they can't pay for them. They offer me corn in exchange. What good is that? I can grow all the corn I need."

"The Legislature should print some paper money, that's what it should do," said another man.

"Gentlemen, gentlemen," said Mr. Webster, who had been listening to the group talking, while he waited for the stagecoach. "The States should *not* print paper money. The national government should buy silver and make dollars, quarters, dimes, that will not shrink in value."

"And where will they get the money to buy the silver, young feller?" answered a graybeard. "Pick it out of the air, ye figger?"

"They must get it from the States in taxes," answered Noah with dignity.

"What, pay taxes here and down in Philadelphia, too? Where will we get the money? I left a leg down in Georgia during the War. I can't scramble after the money as other men can."

"You and many others did a great deal for your country during the War. The finest thing you can do now is to help the States hold together at any cost."

The man with the wooden leg scratched his head reflectively.

" 'Tis a fine country, and no mistake, Stranger," he said. "If the taxes don't swamp us, we'll be glad to pay 'em."

In November a dust-covered young man rode into Hartford on the stagecoach. Noah Webster, the lecturer, returning from eighteen months of travel!

How eagerly his family clustered around him in the red farmhouse, that evening, when he rode out from Hartford on a borrowed horse. They could hardly believe that this impressive person was their own Noah.

"Sakes alive, if it isn't *silk* stockings he wears with his best breeches and coat," said his mother, who was unpacking the saddle-bags. "And buckled slippers, too. You must have brought home a fortune."

"Hardly that, Ma," said Noah sadly. "I needed the good clothes in which to lecture. But I did bring you new ribbons for your bonnet, and a brooch as well. They are only trifles, of course."

"Did the lectures pay well, Son?" asked Mr. Webster. "You wrote that they were well-attended."

"People came to them, and paid me many compliments," answered Noah. "But I have not brought home much money. Enough to live on for a few weeks, and that is all."

"Doubtless the traveling was very expensive."

"It did cost a good deal, Pa."

"Think of the cities you have seen, and the fine folk that live there!" exclaimed his mother. "You will find us very plain people here."

"The best people I know," answered Noah. "There are none finer anywhere."

"Oh, then you are planning to settle down again in Hartford?"

"That I do not know. I must seek a living wherever I can find it. I have written some articles for the *Courant* against the printing of paper money."

"A very good thing, too," said Mr. Webster. "This paper money will be the ruin of us."

"I am glad to hear you say that, Pa. So many men are for it."

"Thoughtless men, surely. Any thinking man can see that paper money must have gold behind it."

"Of course it must," cried Noah. "It has no value without it."

"Come now, speak no more of politics," said Mrs. Webster. "There are apples roasting, and a strip of good venison. I'll have supper on the table in no time."

"As long as I get a piece of cornbread, I will not ask for anything else," answered Noah.

"You may not *ask* for it," said his mother, offended. "But when my son comes home from a year and a half of travel, I hope I can give him something besides corn-bread for supper!"

[146]

CHAPTER NINETEEN

We, the People

ONCE MORE IN the cold of a New England winter Noah Webster started to look for some way to make a living. After talking with friends in Hartford, he decided that it would be hopeless to try to practise law there.

Perhaps there would be something he could do in New York City. Starting off briskly by stagecoach on Thanksgiving Day, 1786, he traveled safely as far as New Haven. Between New Haven and New York, however, the stage-coach broke down, so that he was forced to walk through the snow much of the time during the next four days. Arriving wet and cold in New York, he rented a modest room where he might dry his clothes and spend long evenings in writing. Daytimes he called on various book-sellers and printers, asking for work. He would not have been happy, of course, selling or making books instead of writing them, but he thought he must take whatever came his way. Since no-one offered him any work in the course of the next two weeks, however, he packed his bags once more and started for Philadelphia.

Philadelphia was probably in the back of his mind

from the moment he left Hartford, although he had not definitely planned to go there. Nevertheless, the city drew him like a magnet. Benjamin Franklin and other good friends were in Philadelphia. Fog muffled the city, there was plenty of damp wind, but at least no blanket of snow lay over all the houses.

There were warm fires in Philadelphia, good food and cheerful companions. Also news had spread that a Federal Convention would meet there the following May to patch up the old Articles of Confederation, which held the States loosely together, or to write a new Constitution for the United States. Noah Webster, who liked a finger in every pie, longed to be there. Indeed Benjamin Franklin had written, urging him to come.

Arriving shortly after Christmas, he began energetically making his presence known. Soon the cordial Quakers were inviting him to their houses. The bachelor school-master found himself suddenly quite a social figure.

Dinner in Philadelphia was no simple affair of boiled meat and potatoes. It might begin with turtle soup, go on through lobster or chicken to such delicacies as trifle, whipped sillibub, gooseberry fool, jellies or brandied peaches. After dinner the young people sang together around the harpsichord. Punch and cakes made better late refreshments than the raisins or peppermint candies Noah had eaten late at night in his solitary room in Hartford.

One of the more popular hostesses in Philadelphia at that time was a Mrs. Duncan Ingraham. Mrs. Ingraham's

In the evening the young people sang together around the harpsichord.

young sister, Rebecca Greenleaf, was visiting her that winter. On the first of March, young Mr. Webster, now twenty-eight years old, met Miss Greenleaf. "Becca," as everyone called her, was small, fun-loving and pretty. She adored parties. Since her father was a wealthy merchant in Boston, she had never had to take life very seriously. But Noah Webster wanted her to take *him* seriously. Three weeks after he met her he was calling her "the lovely Becca" in his diary.

Looking anxiously at himself in his steel mirror before going to see her, he wondered if Becca could learn to love him. His face was so solemn and thoughtful. The square chin and high forehead—would she find them attractive? His white neckcloth was slightly yellow from washing; he must get a new one. Some people said that he was vain and strong-willed. In Becca's company he felt the humblest of creatures.

Wildly he wondered if he could make himself over for her—become light-hearted and carefree, less the black crow that he felt and more the handsome peacock. No, his common sense told him that he must remain what he was: a studious young man, anxious to do his duty.

Still, he need not be altogether the dull scholar. In the depths of his gray eyes a spirit of fun twinkled.

In the parlor of Mrs. Ingraham's home, waiting for Becca to come down, Noah felt warm and happy. When she came into the room, he rose and said politely, "You are looking very pretty tonight, Miss Greenleaf."

"Thank you, Mr. Webster. You are looking well yourself."

"General Washington called on me today. I admire him greatly."

"I adore men who do things. So many of the young men here are nothing but social butterflies."

"A man must not have all work and no play in his life either. Such men make dull companions."

"I suppose so. I understand that you sing, Mr. Webster, and play the flute."

"I have not played in some time. I have been much occupied lately with politics. Too much so, I fear."

"Perhaps you would bring your flute some night, and play for me?"

"I would be delighted, Miss Greenleaf."

"I have heard that you know a great deal about politics, Mr. Webster."

"I am passionately interested in the welfare of our country."

"My brother, James, says the United States will become one of the most important countries in the world."

"I am sure of it, if only we have the courage to be truly American. We must not copy other countries, or think of them as better than our own. Our ways are good ways."

"But so many pretty things come from other countries. My brother is an importer, you know. One of his friends, a sea-captain, brought me this lace and this ribbon."

"Someday we will make lace and ribbon as good as any right here in America."

"Oh, fancy wearing bonnet strings that were made in this country!"

"You will wear them someday and be proud of them."

"That *would* be a novelty. But let me get you a drink, Mr. Webster, and a seed-cake. I know seed-cakes are for children, but I adore them."

"You are not much more than a child still, Becca, a lovely, lovable child."

"Me a child! I'll be twenty-one years old on my next birthday!"

"When I was twenty—"

"Way back in the dark ages, I suppose?"

Noah smiled and began again. "When I was twenty, I spent one of the most miserable years of my life, teaching children to read and write in a country school. No child of mine will ever go to such a school, if I can help it."

"But I thought you graduated from Yale College when you were twenty. What were you doing teaching country school after that?"

"I was earning my living the only way I could after the War."

"Oh, I see. And what kind of work do you do now, Mr. Webster?"

"Call me Noah, won't you?"

"Certainly, if you wish it. What kind of work do you do now—Noah?"

"I write books—and lecture—and teach sometimes, too. I have been offered a position here as Master of English in the new Protestant Episcopal Academy."

"That sounds wonderful."

"Not wonderful perhaps, but it would at least enable me to stay on in Philadelphia, where I very much want to be."

"Oh, but that *is* wonderful, I am staying myself until June—another eight weeks at least."

"That is splendid. I will accept the position tomorrow."

And so it was that Noah Webster settled down in Philadelphia to a wonderful springtime of love and happiness. However, it was on no pink cloud of uncertainty that he allowed himself to drift. He was not the man to leave an issue in doubt. Before June he had asked, and received an answer, to the burning question of whether Becca would marry him.

Becca replied that she could not be formally engaged to him until she went home and consulted her father. But in the meantime—between themselves—they might have an "understanding." Becca said that she liked thoughtful, hard-working men. Although her father was wealthy, he had worked hard all his life, building up his business.

Meanwhile, in another part of the city, the delegates to the Federal Convention were at last writing a Constitution for the United States. How Noah trembled, when he thought of the importance of that document. For six years the States had hung together with only the Articles of Confederation to bind them. Now delegates from all over the country were gathered to organize a real national government.

After Becca went back to Boston, Noah concentrated more and more on the Convention. As an outsider, he was not permitted to attend their sessions or to know what was going on behind the closed doors of the convention hall, but in his own peculiar way he took part in the discussion. Not a delegate but had on hand his *Sketches of American Policy,* calling for strong national unity. Not a man but knew that the young schoolmaster was a friend of George Washington, the chairman of the Convention.

For his own part, of course, it was agonizing not to know what decisions were being made. All through the steaming summer, while the delegates worked in absolute secrecy, he fretted and fumed at the delay. George Washington, he knew, was having trouble keeping the members at their great task. There were so many points on which they differed. Would they ever agree on most of them?

Sometimes when he dined, as he frequently did, with George Washington or Benjamin Franklin, he gathered a few crumbs of information. Nor did he merely listen to what others were saying at these dinners. At the smallest break in the conversation, he plunged in with his own passionate opinion of what the country needed. A newspaper editor, who did not like him, wrote of him spitefully early in the summer, "He slaps his merits in our teeth." But Webster was no man to hesitate, when he felt that the good of the country was at stake. Firmly on every possible occasion, he said what he thought should be put into the new Constitution.

Somehow the long summer passed. On the seventeenth of September thirty-nine hot and weary men brought forth the document on which they had been working.

We, the people of the United States, in order to form a more perfect Union, establish justice, insure domestic tranquility, provide for the common defence, promote the general welfare, and secure the blessings of liberty to ourselves and our posterity, do ordain and establish this Constitution for the United States of America.

CHAPTER TWENTY

The Magazine That Failed

THE NEW CONSTITUTION of the United States was all that Noah Webster had hoped for. A strong, simple agreement, binding the separate States together in a "more perfect Union." At last there would be national government in America.

But before the Constitution became law, at least nine States must ratify it. And there were still men in all the thirteen States who did not want national government. The thought that some of these men might hinder the adoption of the Constitution filled Webster with anguish. Something—everything—must be done to prevent this calamity from occurring.

Seizing the weapon that came most readily to his hand —a sharpened goose quill—he dipped fiercely into the ink. Every possible question that anyone might ask about the new Constitution must be answered carefully. A pamphlet, giving this information, must be sent into every corner of the country.

Freeing himself from his teaching, he covered many pages with his beautiful, clear logic. It was October now, cool and crisp, but he was far from cool or crisp when he finished his labor. In two days he had written what other men might have taken a month to write.

The name of his pamphlet, like all his other titles, was a bit resounding. *An Examination into the Leading Principles of the Federal Constitution proposed by the late Convention held at Philadelphia.* The signature, however, was not resounding at all. Webster signed himself simply, *A Citizen of America,* and dedicated his work to Benjamin Franklin.

A week after it was finished, the pamphlet was published and on its way to every part of the United States. Doubtful men everywhere read it. They became convinced that it was right for the separate States to bow to the national government "in all matters of a general nature." The army, the navy, the postal service, the printing of money, all must be handled by a central authority. There was still no Capitol for the United States, no White House, no President, no Congress, no Post Office, no Mint, but these would come later. The important thing now was for the separate States to ratify the Constitution. Until that was done, Noah could not rest. But in writing his pamphlet he had done all that he could to bring it about.

Meanwhile the young schoolmaster, now twenty-nine years old, must earn his living and prepare a home for the young wife he hoped to marry. A man on horseback, going from city to city, would not make a good husband. Neither could he go back to country school-teaching, after his years of writing and lecturing. The royalties on his Spelling Book and Reader were not large enough to support a family. The truth was that he was still not out of debt to his father, although he had lived frugally and worked hard. Once more he must decide what he should do to earn his living.

After looking into various possibilities, Webster decided to start a new magazine in New York City. This decision took courage. Already in debt, he must find money with which to pay for his magazine. If it failed to win subscribers, he would lose whatever money he put into it. If it made money, however, he would be able to marry "that good girl," Rebecca Greenleaf.

Spurred on by love, Webster rushed recklessly at his new venture. His first move was to sell the publishing rights to his Spelling Book and Reader in New York, New Jersey, and three southern States for two hundred dollars. This was shockingly bad business. The man who bought the rights sold 200,000 copies of the books. If he had paid a penny on each copy, Webster would have received two thousand dollars during the five years, instead of two hundred dollars at the beginning. If he had paid two-and-a-half cents a copy, which was what his Boston publisher paid him, Webster would have received five thousand dollars during the five years. Such a contract would have solved most of his financial problems for a long time. But who could say that the Spelling Book would sell so prodigiously in the southern States, where there were still almost no schools?

And so, on two hundred dollars, Webster started *The American Magazine.* From the beginning it was popular. The young editor filled his magazine with ripe plums of wisdom on many subjects: government, literature, education, agriculture and philology. If he preached at them a little, his readers forgave him. The only difficulty was that there were not too many readers. The people of the United States did not read magazines very freely at that time. The few subscriptions that came in barely paid the cost of printing the magazine.

Indeed, as the year wore on, Webster found himself dipping into the modest royalties from his books to pay for his magazine. Instead of the magazine feeding him, he was feeding the magazine. To a young man who hoped to marry, this would never do. With a sigh of relief in October, 1788, shortly before his thirtieth birthday, Noah gave up his magazine.

"30 years of my life gone!" he wrote in his diary on his birthday. "I have read much, written much, tried to do much good, but with little advantage to myself. I will now leave writing."

To Becca in Boston, he wrote more eagerly. "I am happy to quit New York," he said, and she could guess the reason why.

From New York Webster went directly to Boston to see Rebecca. A year and a half had passed since she said good-by to him in Philadelphia. Would she be the same merry, brown-eyed girl? She was that, and more now. Proudly she told him that she was learning to cook and sew, that she would rather mend than embroider. Noah, however, was determined not to marry her until he could support her properly. To her brother, James, he wrote: "I would not think of marrying her until I can take her to a pleasant home and spread a decent table for her friends."

Just what it was that Rebecca needed to make her happy, he was not sure. Pretty bonnets, fancy furniture, delicacies for the table? He himself was quite unused to luxury. But whatever it was that she needed, he meant to supply it. The only question was how.

Reluctantly in May he left Boston for Hartford, to see if he could find a little legal work there. Surely now that he was known as both a writer and lecturer, clients would come. Enough of them came during the summer for him to be distinctly encouraged. With the royalties due from his books during the next two years—five or six hundred dollars a year—might he not hope to support a family? If Rebecca was willing, how happy they could be!

Rebecca was entirely willing. In fact, she could hardly wait to marry her sober young schoolmaster and have her own pretty home in Hartford. Her brother, James, had given them a thousand dollars with which to buy furniture. She was twenty-three now, old enough to manage everything nicely. If Noah would come to Boston, they could be married almost immediately.

The first thing that Becca bought for her new home was an expensive mirror. Then she bought dishes and chintz chairs for the dining-room. Carpets and curtains were of the very best quality. Her wedding dress came next, with a new cloak and bonnet and slippers. She was much startled one evening to have Noah bring her a list of her purchases with the prices marked after them. The money, he said, was now gone—indeed more than gone. And there was still no furniture for the parlor, nor pots and pans for the kitchen.

"How can that be, Noah?" she asked. "A thousand dollars should buy everything we can possibly need."

"It can buy a lot," said Noah, "but not everything we can think of."

"Oh, I have been a very foolish girl," cried Becca, beginning to weep on his shoulder. "I have spoiled everything."

"Not everything, my dear. Only your chance to have a pretty parlor."

"I can wait for that!" answered Becca. "But I want to be a good wife to you!"

"Well, then, dry your eyes, and say you'll marry me anyhow."

"Of course I'll marry you," answered Becca, who had a cheerful nature, and could not be downhearted long.

The wedding took place on October 26th in her father's home. Noah's family did not come to it. The fact that he was marrying a wealthy girl from Boston made them feel far away from him. Besides, if they did come, who would milk the cows and feed the hens in their absence?

Ten days later Mr. and Mrs. Noah Webster moved into their new home in Hartford, "a large, convenient, elegant house" Noah wrote in his diary, a house in which to make pies and puddings for her husband, as Rebecca told herself happily.

The parlor was a little bare, but the kitchen was warm and cheerful that autumn. The pots and pans, gathered together somehow, were never empty. Rebecca made plum puddings and pumpkin puddings. In one day she baked seven apple pies. Noah Webster, who had always been a finicky eater, ate her pies and puddings with relish.

Friends came to dine, and remained to talk politics, while the ladies bent over their sewing. Webster joined a literary club, and met most of the prominent men in Hartford. But still a small voice whispered that he was not making enough money to cover their expenses, and that he still owed his father money.

Thanksgiving Day the young couple drove out to West Hartford for dinner with Noah's family. How the children crowded around their new "Aunt Becca," in her green brocade dress covered with pink and red roses.

Her bonnet was more beautiful than any they had ever seen.

Mrs. Webster cried and hugged Rebecca, when she met her. This little lady her Noah's wife! It hardly seemed possible.

Noah beamed upon them all, and took a second helping of turkey, when they were gathered around the table.

"Lord bless me, he'll have some meat on his bones yet," cried his mother. "What have you done to him, Becca, to make him relish his victuals so?"

"The turkey is delicious; no-one could help wanting more," answered Rebecca modestly. But seeing Noah's clear eyes and fresh coloring, she was proud of her care of him.

Throughout the meal, Noah's father said very little. After helping the little ones generously, and dishing the last spoonful of gravy, he sat quietly staring at a mug of cider.

"Come now, have ye naught to say to the little lady?" asked his wife, trying to rally him.

" 'Tis welcome ye are here. The boy and all know that," he answered. And that was all he said until the meal was over.

While the young people were washing the dishes, and Mrs. Webster sat stiffly in the parlor in honor of her guest, Mr. Webster drew Noah into the bedroom.

"I have no wish to spoil your day, Son," he said. "But

I must tell ye something. An attachment has been laid against this farm. In a few weeks I shall lose it."

"Oh, Pa!" cried Noah. "And all because I never paid back the money I borrowed from you."

"That money was well spent," said Mr. Webster firmly. "It put your feet on the right path. But before the new year your mother and I will be gone from here."

"Where will you go, Pa? What will you do?"

"We are going over into New York State to the new settlements," said Mr. Webster. "There is land to be had there."

"I can't believe that you will no longer be here. This place has been home to me as long as I can remember."

"And anxious ye were to leave it, ever since ye were shaver, eh, my boy?"

"I wanted education, and to make my way in the world. But you and Ma belong here."

"The man who owns it now figgers different. We'll be out of here before Christmas."

"Then this is my last Thanksgiving in the old home!"

"Your first likewise with the little lady. Take care o her, Son. She's worth it."

"I will, Pa. I will. And God bless you on the new land."

CHAPTER TWENTY-ONE

More Writing and Editing

I N HIS QUIET law office Noah spent many days that winter busily writing. He was writing now for little children. Already in Philadelphia in 1786 he had published a new and more cheerful edition of the gloomy *New England Primer* out of which, as a child of five or six, he had learned his own letters. The older book began thus:

A
In Adam's Fall
We sinned all.

Webster's revision began thus:

A Was an Apple-pie made by the cook.
B Was a Boy that was fond of his book.

The next book which he wrote was a simple grammar for young children, called *Rudiments of English Grammar*. This book was notable, not for its rules of grammar, but for a little essay at the end, called "A Federal Catechism." This explained for the first time the new American Constitution. Nowadays, when everyone studies our national government as a matter of course in history classes, it would be startling to find this information in the back of a grammar. But in Webster's time, when history was not taught at all, it was considered a great novelty.

The next book which he wrote was a reader called *The Little Reader's Assistant*. Here he included twenty-two short tales, describing the adventures of Christopher Columbus, John Smith and Pocahontas, and the early settlers of New England. He also described the hardships suffered by Negro slaves in the South.

Altogether there were six little books in the series Webster wrote at this time They were the first schoolbooks for young children, published anywhere, that gave some American history and geography. Webster sang the praises of America for the first time. The song, "My country, 'tis of thee," had not yet been written, but it might have been written about his books.

> My country, 'tis of thee,
> Sweet land of liberty,
> Of thee I sing.

How truly he might have said these words, as he labored quietly in his law office in Hartford during the early years of his marriage.

The next book which he wrote began as a series of essays to run in the *Connecticut Courant* for twenty-eight weeks, beginning in December, 1790. This series was published the following autumn under the general title of *The Prompter*.

"A Prompter," he wrote, "is the man who in plays sits behind the scenes, looks over the rehearser, and with a moderate voice corrects him when he is wrong. A Prompter says but *little,* but that little is necessary, and often does much *good. . . .*"

"The Prompter's business," he continued, "is with common things. A dish of highly-seasoned turtle is rarely found. . . . But good solid roast beef is a common dish for all men; it sits easy on the stomach. . . . Vulgar sayings and proverbs are the roast beef of science."

This dish of roast beef, which he set before the public in 1791, was widely enjoyed.

Meanwhile, the law practice, which he hoped would come to him if he were patient, developed very slowly. Four years slipped by—busy and happy years during which he went a little deeper into debt all the time! It was not until the summer of 1793, that he realized that something must be done about this.

Behind the house where the Webster family lived, there was a small garden. Here Noah grew and experimented with vegetables, working usually for an hour before breakfast or in the late afternoon after he came home from his office. Digging energetically in this garden one July morning, he found himself turning over in his mind certain unpleasant facts. The first was that his law practice was shrinking instead of growing. The second was that he owed more money now than he had ever owed in his life before. Two hundred dollars, borrowed in order to buy law books, three or four hundred in unpaid bills, added to what he still owed his father, brought the total up to an uncomfortable figure. Moreover, the Webster family was growing: two little girls had been born in the four years since he married Rebecca. His expenses were bound to grow as his family expanded.

Plunging his spade firmly into the earth, he looked at the other side of the picture. In the four years since he came back to Hartford to live, he had done his best to be a good citizen. He had been elected to the Common Council of the city, and had worked hard to get new paving for the streets, new gutters and canals where they were needed. Through his law club, he had helped to collect money for a new state house. He had written articles for the paper, urging accident insurance for workmen injured at their jobs.

He had worked actively in the local anti-slavery society. He had been commissioned by the Postmaster General to catch a thief, who was robbing the mail between New York City and Hartford, and after much work succeeded in finding the guilty man. Besides his six little textbooks for young children, he had published two large books, *A Collection of Essays and Fugitive Writings,* which demanded an American spelling, and *The Prompter.*

Any man, he thought angrily, who had done all this, should be able to earn a living somehow. Yet the bald truth remained, that if he were ever to pay his debts, he must give up practising law in Hartford.

With Noah Webster to think was to act. Flinging down his spade, he marched into the house and said that he was going to Boston either to publish books or take over a book store. Mrs. Webster heard this news with dismay. He seemed too much a scholar and writer for that. The quantity of writing he did habitually every day was almost frightening.

For a second choice, Noah said, he would take up farming. This idea did not please Mrs. Webster either. It was true, she said, that he had grown up on a farm, and knew how to cut hay and plant potatoes. But the need to say what he thought on paper was strong in him. Given a whole day of farming he would probably be found at midday in a fence-corner, reading or writing an article for some newspaper. Even as a boy, she reminded him, he had studied Latin out under the apple-trees in his father's orchard, when he should have been plowing.

"I hope," said her husband with dignity, "that as a grown man I can be counted on to do my duty."

"Of course, dear, I did not mean that," said Rebecca hastily. "I am only saying that you must do the work that you were born to do. Otherwise you would be unhappy."

"Well, if it is not to be farming, why not the book-selling?" persisted Noah. "Wouldn't you like to live in Boston again, where your old friends are?"

"Until you got started at the book-selling, we would

have to live very modestly in Boston, wouldn't we?" said Rebecca.

There it was again. The fact that he had married a rich girl who must now live in the plainest fashion! Rebecca made a good wife and mother; she cooked and sewed for her family indefatigably. But of course she wanted pretty clothes and a chance to go to parties. A pity she had married a solemn owl of a scholar.

But Rebecca did not think she was to be pitied. She adored her scholar. She would not have him different. It was merely that she wanted him to keep on writing and writing until his fame spread to every hamlet in the country. In the end, Noah Webster went to New York City to edit a new daily paper, called *The American Minerva.*

What a change that was to plunge into the life of a great city after the peaceful life of Hartford. So many people to meet, so much to see and do. In his diary, after all the other work of the day, Noah wrote down his impressions. His keen eye went everywhere, there was no landmark or museum he did not visit. On a previous visit to New York City he had even counted the houses, sixteen hundred of them, going up one street and down another until he had counted them all!

As an editor he worked frantically, writing articles for the paper. Newspaper editing in those days was a robust business. Writers did not merely state their opinions in their articles; they attacked the other fellow in the most vigorous language. Whoever disagreed with Noah called him all sorts of names. "See-saw editor," "spiteful viper," "toad," "fool" and "barefaced liar" were all hurled at his head. But the sharp sword of his reasoning cut deeply, too. In the lively battles of words he more than held his own.

Altogether, in the five years that he was in New York, Noah Webster wrote enough to fill twenty large volumes. Not that the material was ever gathered together and published that way. Newspaper articles are meant to be read on the day they are published. The flood of today's words washes away the flood of yesterday's.

Noah Webster enjoyed saying what he thought on every subject, but a small voice whispered sometimes that he could not keep it up forever. Other subjects, not suitable for newspaper articles, needed discussing, too. The subject of infectious diseases, for instance, which took so many lives during every epidemic. His own children had been desperately ill one year with scarlet fever. His brother had almost died of smallpox when he was in the army. Yellow fever came regularly to every city. What caused these epidemics? How should these diseases be treated?

Doctors frankly disagreed as to both the cause and cure for epidemics. Some doctors said the smoke of burning tar was helpful for yellow fever; others laughed at this treatment. Some said dead animals and garbage should not be left in the streets; others said that this had nothing to do with sickness. Whenever he thought about these things, Noah Webster became again the walking question-mark he had been as a student at Yale College. If he could only get away to some quiet place, and write to every doctor in the country about his experience with infectious diseases, some light might be thrown on the whole question. Instead of which, he was wrestling with dishonest printers, writing thousands of words each day which lay the next day on the scrap-heap like so much unwanted garbage.

Already in the year 1795 he had begun collecting letters from physicians on their experiences with epidemic diseases. By the spring of 1798 this material was choking his office. It could not be thrown together hastily and published in a daily newspaper. It should be analyzed and examined carefully. The scent of new knowledge was strong in Noah Webster's nostrils. With a sigh of relief, he gave up his post as editor and made plans to move his family to New Haven.

CHAPTER TWENTY-TWO

Nine Years in New Haven

THE NEW HOUSE in New Haven was more like the home Rebecca and Noah Webster had dreamed of than any since their marriage. A spacious white house, facing the harbor; an orchard and garden behind it; a stable for the horse; neighbors who lived as they did.

There were three little girls in the Webster family now. During the next ten years three more little girls and a son came to join them. Noah himself would have welcomed more children. He said ten made a nice number.

Becca, with seven now in her brood, found herself always busy. The little girls must be taught to cook and sew, to sing and play on the harpsichord. Papa must have the quiet he needed in order to do his writing. Twice a day the children might go with him to the postoffice. The rest of the day they must tiptoe and whisper when they passed his door.

"Sh-h, Papa is working," little Emily would explain to the most important visitor, who came unexpectedly at noontime. At four o'clock, however, Mama opened the door of his room boldly, with a plate of fruit and cake in her hand. This meant that they could go into the strange room with its piles and piles of papers, and climb on his knee, and search his pockets for peppermints. When he dug in the garden, too, they might hold the packets of seeds for him, and hear him talk about the birds and flowers. Papa had grown up on a farm, and knew a great deal about plants and animals. He was writing a book now about sickness, but he liked to have his lively, healthy family around him when the day's writing was finished.

Papa said that all his life he had waited for just such a home as this, with just such a family. The only thing he needed now was a better dictionary with all the words he needed in it!

Mama said that Papa was an "OMNIVOROUS" student and reader. Already he knew many more words than he could find in any dictionary. He had taught himself several new languages lately, and read in Hebrew or Greek or Latin as easily as they did in their well-thumbed primers. It was hard not to be a little afraid of Papa, when he wore his writing face. But when he took that face off at sunset, and smiled out of his wide-awake gray eyes under the bushy eyebrows, they could ask him about anything. There was no other child in all New Haven whose father knew as much about everything as did Papa Webster!

The love of his children during the next nine years meant much to Noah Webster because his work did not always go well, or win the approval which he hoped for it. Toiling earnestly day after day, he produced during his first two years in New Haven a vast book on infectious diseases from material gathered from many doctors. Wherever smallpox, or yellow fever or influenza struck, he wrote the local doctors, asking questions about it. What was the climate like, the atmosphere, the altitude, the geography? What treatment had they used? What opinion did they have?

Nowadays we know that most of that work was wasted. A microscope, which nobody dreamed of using, would have shown germs, which no-one knew existed. Questions about the water supply and the disposal of garbage would have been more revealing than questions about the air in the sickroom. How many mosquitoes and flies were there in the neighborhood? No-one thought to ask that. So two years' work, and the expense of publishing his report, was wasted.

Not quite wasted, however, for in his inquiry into diseases lay the seeds of Webster's greatest work of all, the book he sat down to write when he was nearly fifty.

The fact was that he was bothered all through his years of scientific investigation by the lack of a suitable dictionary. Incredible as it may seem now, the dictionaries of that day contained almost no scientific words. Webster bought and consulted them all, without finding in them dozens of words which every schoolboy and girl knows today. Patiently he searched—in the library at Yale College, in Philadelphia, in New York, in Boston, for books which would give him the definitions he wanted. What he found chiefly were essays by Latin authors on the affairs of Rome many centuries before America was discovered.

The more he searched the more impatient he grew. Whenever he found a word, which was not in any dictionary, he jotted it down and defined it himself. The piles of notes in his study filled all the chairs and tables. No-one must go in there to dust: supposing they disturbed some of the papers? Rebecca, who had a proper respect for his notebooks, left her mending to try to help him with his papers. She was clever at it, too. Just one more reason, he thought, for loving the charming woman he had married.

The best dictionary of that day, of course, was Dr. Samuel Johnson's—two large books seventeen inches long and three inches thick. Surely no-one could look there and find any omissions. Dr. Johnson had worked for eight years on this dictionary, which was published in 1755, three years before Noah Webster was born. It held over fifty thousand words.

After months of studying this dictionary, however, Noah Webster was prepared to criticize it heartily. It held, he said, pages of quotations from forgotten authors. It made many mistakes in giving the history of words from foreign languages. Webster himself by the time he was fifty had learned twelve languages; in another six years he knew twenty.

The more languages he learned, the more difficult it was for him to keep his reference books in order. Finally he had a huge table built in the shape of a half circle, with books around the entire rim. He could thus work from the right-hand corner to the left, tracing one word in many languages.

Worst of all the faults of Dr. Johnson's dictionary, however, was the fact it did not contain one word of information on the American Revolution or the new United States. It did not contain, either, many good Yankee words like "shaver" for small boy, "chores" for daily duties, "miff" for quarrel, "tackle" for harness, and "whittle" for shaving a piece of wood. It was distressing, too, to Noah Webster as a farmer's son. to see the word "tallow" defined simply as "animal fat," when everyone knew that it was fat only from sheep or oxen. Fat from swine should be called lard or suet.

By the year 1800 Noah Webster knew that he must write a good English dictionary as his lifework. By the year 1807 he had freed himself enough of other work to begin working constantly on it.

The years from 1800 to 1807 were not altogether happy ones. When his book on infectious diseases was published a great many people made fun of it. The first dictionary which he published, too, in 1806, was roundly criticized. People asked who this country school teacher was who dared to criticize Dr. Samuel Johnson. He had actually left out of his dictionary certain of Dr. Johnson's words—

words like *decumbiture* and *fishefy,* which no-one used any more, but still were accustomed to find in dictionaries. Webster's spelling, too, was different from the old English spelling. He spelled *honour* as *honor, thumb* as *thum, feather* as *fether,* and *axe* as *ax.* He also included the word *soapy.* No-one ever put that in a dictionary before!

Patiently in his prefaces, and in articles in newspapers, Webster explained that language was a living, changing thing—not something fixed and finished for all time. Some people agreed with him in this; others took pains to call him foolish.

By this time, however, Noah Webster was used to criticism. The world and its hasty judgment no longer distressed him. The quiet room where he worked made a sanctuary around him. The truth, as he saw it, went steadily into his writing.

Meanwhile, he did not forget that the boys and girls of America needed schoolbooks. The days were long past when children read only in the Bible, but there were still many subjects on which they needed instruction. Webster's own children were getting too big now for his Spelling Book and Reader. When he first came to New Haven they had needed even a schoolhouse, but their father soon saw to that. Calling together a group of citizens, he organized a Union School, built of brick, with two comfortable rooms in it. No drafty cabin with a dirt floor would do for his little girls. But if he had seen the schools in America today, with their classrooms, offices, and gymnasiums, he would indeed have opened his eyes!

Webster had in mind four textbooks under the general title, *Elements of Useful Knowledge.* The first two gave a "Historical and Geographical Account of the United States." The third contained "A Historical and Geographical Account of Europe, Asia and Africa," the fourth contained "A History of Animals." Thus geography, history and biology were for the first time offered to school-children so long nourished in the three Rs, Reading, Writing and 'Rithmetic. The days were definitely past when a Connecticut farmer could say, as he said once when Noah first began teaching: "All I want my boys to learn is the Bible and figgers!"

The first nine years in New Haven were now definitely over. During them Noah Webster had accomplished an incredible amount of work. The two volumes on infectious diseases had been written and published. Four textbooks and a dictionary had been produced. He had learned half a dozen new languages. This man lived and swam in words. If a day went by when he did not tussle with a new definition, or find a new word in a foreign language, he was unhappy.

CHAPTER TWENTY-THREE

D for Declaration

Now IT COULD not be put off any longer. Noah Webster must write a good American dictionary.

A man nearly fifty years old, ruddy and strong, with a growing family around him, sat down early one morning to begin his great task. The year was 1807. The place: New Haven, one of the most beautiful cities in the United States.

Breakfast that morning was much like every other breakfast. Coffee and toast and "relish"—the Webster family ate simple, nourishing meals. Then the brisk walk to the postoffice, after which the door of his room closed behind him. From that moment until a January morning nearly twenty years later Noah Webster worked on the greatest book he ever wrote, *An American Dictionary of the English Language.*

His working habits were by now fixed and unalterable. The machinery of his home moved on oiled wheels. Gone the days when Rebecca Webster, as a young girl, had bought mirrors but no parlor sofa with her wedding money. Gone the days, too, when she "bawled" over a cake that would not rise or baked more apple pies than her husband could eat in a week.

With five little girls and a son around her, she spent her days cheerily going from one task to another. The new baby who came the following year completed her family.

True, money was not plentiful in the Webster household. It had never been plentiful. Book after book had been published with the cost paid out of Noah Webster's own pocket. Valuable time had been spent writing newspaper articles which said a great deal, but did not bring in much money. If Webster had written often, and strongly, about the need for national banks and stable money, it was partly because he had himself suffered so often from seeing his dollars melt away with nothing.

While he was writing the dictionary the family must live on the royalties that came in from the faithful Spelling Book and Reader. These books had sold enormously. They were still selling at a good rate. But at half a cent a copy, which was his average royalty, a great many copies must be sold to bring in even a few dollars. Sometimes he got as much as a penny a copy for the books. Other times he got less than half a cent. The Spelling Book sold a great deal better than the Reader. When the sales reached 200,000 copies a year, which they often did, Webster received $1,000. On this sum he intended living while he completed his dictionary.

A sailor loves the sea. A carpenter loves his tools. A

writing man loves his paper and pens, and the words that sing in his head during the day. Sometimes the words are rambunctious and refuse to fit into their proper places. A definition may be as elusive as a fish avoiding the hook. But Noah Webster was prepared to wrestle with them all indefatigably, until he had defined every word in the American language.

Help, of course, he would receive from dictionaries which had been published earlier. Every dictionary is bound to build on the dictionaries that come before it. Already Webster knew by heart the early English books of "hard words," which were the first dictionaries ever published. The first of these books, *The Table Alphabeticall of Hard Words,* published in 1600, contained only 3,000 words, words like *bubulcitate* meaning to "cry like a cowboy," as well as others no longer used anywhere. There was a dictionary by John Walker, published in 1791, which said that it was polite to pronounce the word, *garden* as *g-yarden,* and *guard* as *g-yard.*

This kind of elegance made Webster very impatient. He even quoted from famous authors to show that it was proper to say *I come home yesterday,* instead of *I came home yesterday.* But on the whole, he decided it was better to have *came* in the language!

There would be scientific words in his dictionary, too, scores of them never heard in Dr. Johnson's time. When people stopped to consider, they realized that Noah Webster was very well qualified to write a dictionary. He knew nearly two dozen languages. He had read all the prominent Latin and Greek and Hebrew authors in college. He had studied and practised law. He had an intimate knowledge of medical terms from his study of infectious diseases. He had written about politics and business for years at a time. He had written textbooks about history, geography and biology. He had traveled over all the thirteen United States, hearing the New England drawl in Connecticut, the accent of Pennsylvania Dutch farmers, the Southern planters in Virginia, shrewd businessmen in New York. Hardly a man in America at that time had more exact knowledge on more subjects than he did.

When it came to American affairs, of course, he was in his own well-loved field. He was only too happy to add words like *land-office, plantation, senate, congress* and *assembly* to his lists.

"No person in this country," he wrote in his preface to the dictionary, "will be satisfied with the English definitions of those words." He also wrote in the preface that the stirring words of Franklin, Washington, Adams, Jay, etc., "should be placed as authorities on the same page with Boyle, Hooker, Milton, Dryden and Cowper."

With what pride, too, did he write when he came to the Ds:

"Declaration: a public annunciation, as the *Declaration of Independence,* July 4, 1776."

"He does love to dress up in your things and strut up and down."

Midday dinner interrupted his work but shortly. The vegetables, which they ate, grew in his own garden. For dessert, fruit sufficed. Then back to his semi-circular table, until Mrs. Webster came in at four o'clock.

After years of training, of course, the children knew that Papa must not be disturbed in his book-filled room. The papers and notebooks, which lay on all the chairs and tables, were sacred, too. A dreadful thing it was, if a careless child upset one of these piles of papers, or hurried past the table in such a way as to blow a paper from its place. Even the cat seemed to know that she must creep around this room discreetly.

But a clever child knew, too, that at four o'clock Papa would have his fill of writing. Peeping cautiously in at the open door, they saw him lay down his pen with a sigh of satisfaction, and remove his glasses. While Papa ate his fruit and cake the little girls and their brother, William, sucked peppermints from a dish on the mantel. After that they might sit on his knee, admiring his wonderful hair and ruddy complexion.

Rising presently, he would say briskly, "Come now, a little fresh air is good for man and beast. Becca, Becca, where is my hat and stick?"

"Yes, dear, do you want something?" she would answer, coming quickly to the door.

"My hat and stick! Never in the same place! I find it very exasperating."

"I'm afraid William has been playing with them again. He does love to dress up in your things and strut up and down."

"When I was a boy I wouldn't have dreamed of touching my father's things. Children nowadays have no proper respect for their elders."

But there was a twinkle in his eyes when he said this.

"Hurry, dear," said Mama, tying a small bonnet under Mary's or Eliza's chin. "If you are going walking with Papa you must not keep him waiting."

The bigger girls, Emily and Julia and Harriet, stood smiling in the doorway.

They were a happy family together—the Websters, the mother so gay and energetic and practical, the father lost in his dreams of words, but devoted and gentle and gallant.

CHAPTER TWENTY-FOUR

Birdsong in Springtime

THE REAL TEST of the family affection came in the year 1812, when Noah Webster came out of his room one afternoon and announced to his horrified family that they could no longer remain in the comfortable white house in New Haven.

"We must move to the country—to Amherst in Massachusetts," he said calmly. "We can no longer afford to live here. I shall farm as well as write there."

"Amherst! Why, that is only a small village!" cried Julia, who knew a boy in New Haven whom she liked very much.

"Yes, quite a small village," said her father, "but I trust we can be happy there."

Emily and Julia burst into tears. Even Mrs. Webster looked anxious.

"Must we really sell our home here, Noah?" she asked. "Can you not borrow the money we need until your Dictionary is completed?"

"I have borrowed too much already," said Noah. "Further loans are out of the question."

"Yes, of course, dear. I was only thinking of the girls and their young men."

"I am sorry about that," said the father. "But there is no help for it. We must live very modestly during the next years."

"Of course, dear," answered Mrs. Webster dutifully.

With great reluctance the trunks were brought down and packed, the dishes put in boxes, everything lifted into the cart that was to carry their goods to Amherst.

And where and what was Amherst, thought the girls a little rebelliously? A tiny village in a valley, with the Green Mountains around it. A farming village with perhaps two hundred and fifty houses in it. Few beaux for the girls. Few neighbors with whom Mama could enjoy a good afternoon chat. Few men with whom Papa could spend an evening in sober talk.

The new house, however, was nice. Large and plain with ten acres of meadow around it. While the girls and Mrs. Webster unpacked and settled the furniture, Noah himself got in the hay for winter, bought cows, made plans for fruit and vegetable gardens. In his heart he was glad to be back in this rural community. It reminded him of his boyhood on the quiet farm in West Hartford. He had not wanted to stay on the farm, but he never hated farm life. There was something about looking out over broad fields in the morning that put a man in the mood to work.

The room in which he wrote was now also his bedroom. How clear his mind was when he woke at daybreak in the frosty fall weather. He remembered a story about Benjamin Franklin, how he used to wake at four or five in the morning and, rising immediately, write letters in his cold room for an hour before breakfast. Long before the family was stirring, Noah Webster was up and about his room, laying out the day's work.

Altogether nine years flew by in Amherst, before Webster reached the letter H in his Dictionary. He himself was hardly conscious of their passing, although many changes came to his family during that time. The three oldest girls, Emily and Julia and Harriet, married—Emily and Julia to the very young men they had left behind in New Haven! Grandchildren came to prattle at Grandpa's knee, and to learn anew that his closed door was sacred.

Then Mary, the liveliest of them all, the one who had walked and driven with him oftenest, married, and died a year later, leaving a little daughter, Mary, behind her. Mr. and Mrs. Webster brought the baby girl home to live with them.

William, the son, got himself into and out of trouble a number of times. Louisa, the youngest daughter, was seriously ill, and never quite well again.

A college was needed in Amherst, where young men might study for the ministry. Webster helped to found it. The music at the First Church was lagging. The Webster family took charge of it. There was no Sunday School for the grandchildren. Webster got one started. Somehow the old life in New Haven slipped into the background, with everyone busy and happy in Amherst or gone to new homes of their own.

By the summer of 1822 Webster had been working fifteen years on his Dictionary. Another three years, he thought, would see him through. Moreover, he had done all the work that he could in a spot remote from libraries. Without hesitation that summer he moved his family back to New Haven to a small house at the corner of College and Wall Streets. There he worked for another year, before building a new house in a better location.

The trees around the new house were full of birdsong in the springtime. Listening to them in the morning made it easy for him to write about them. He had reached the Ws now. Only four more letters to the alphabet.

"Warble, v.t. & i.," he wrote. "To sing or utter in a trilling, quavering or vibratory manner."

So much for the verb. But there was more to be added.

"Warble, n." he continued, remembering long hours and days in the saddle when he was younger. "A hard tumor on a horse's back, due to the heat or pressure of the saddle."

Then back to the birds again—was it a blue-throat or reed warbler singing now outside his window?

"Warbler," he wrote, taking a fresh quill and concentrating. "Any of a family (Sylviidae) of small Old World singing birds, including the blue-throat, white-throat, reed warbler, etc." Also "Any of a large family (Mniotiltidae) of American insectivorous singing birds (collectively called wood warblers), mostly very small and bright-colored."

This information about the birds came from various sources, but the thrill that came with it was all part of his boyhood. How long it was now, since he was a farm-lad out in the early morning, plowing a straight furrow and feeling the spring come back to a cold New England hillside after the winter snow.

CHAPTER TWENTY-FIVE

A Neat Figure in Smallclothes

IN THE SUMMER of the year 1824, Noah Webster found that he had defined all the words that he could without consulting books which were not in the United States. Obviously, then, he must go where the books were, even though they were far away in France and England. A four weeks' voyage was required to reach them. He had no money for his expenses. Nevertheless, in June he borrowed a thousand dollars from one of his daughters and set sail, at the ripe age of sixty-five, for France.

Crossing the ocean in those days was no matter of a few days on a luxury liner. The ship, the *Edward Quesnel,* on which Webster and his son, William, embarked, was a small sailing-vessel, bound for Havre, France. Nineteen other passengers sailed with them. Four of the nineteen were ladies, but William complained that three of them were "old and ugly as witches." With the one pretty lady he must enjoy himself as best he could.

The ship skimmed along through rough seas and smooth for many days. The cabins were small and stuffy. Three times a day platters of wretched food were put on a long table in the saloon. Benjamin Franklin, who had crossed the ocean many times, had warned Webster of the discomforts of travel. How uncomfortable it would be, however, he had not imagined. Yet forty years ago he had ridden a horse for days at a time in all sorts of weather on his journeys around the country. Surely now he could put up with a few weeks of heaving ocean and unpalatable food. But he was very glad to reach Havre at last, and begin the journey by stagecoach to Paris.

The stagecoach itself was a heavy vehicle drawn by six horses. Webster looked at them critically.

"Why, they are not fit even for plowing!" he said to William, thinking of his own trim mare at home. "As for the harness, it is downright disgraceful!"

"I have always heard that everything in France was very elegant," murmured William.

"Certainly the means of travel are not," answered his father. "We will see what the inns are like."

The hotels, however, were equally disappointing. Rude porters, damp beds, dingy linen. How he longed for the comfort of his own home in New Haven, with clever Rebecca looking after his every need.

Nevertheless, in time the two travelers reached Paris, and found tolerable lodgings. After that they began to enjoy themselves. On July 24 Webster entered the royal library, the Bibliotheque de Roi as it was called, and saw there 800,000 books gathered together. The sight fairly stunned him.

"In America," he said to William, "in all the college libraries, there are scarcely 80,000 books."

"Even that number seems enough," answered William, who was no scholar like his father. "You told me once that when you first went to Yale, and saw twenty-five hundred books in the library there, you were overcome with emotion."

"That was fifty years ago, when I was not yet sixteen," answered his father with dignity. "America still needs many more books."

"I suppose so," answered William. "Tell me what are you planning to do here? Even you cannot read 800,000 books, Papa."

"I came to look up scientific terms," answered Noah. "Some of them have no American equivalents. In time, of course, there will be an American word for everything."

"Won't the French words do, if Frenchmen invented them?"

"Perhaps in certain cases. In general, there should be an American translation for every French phrase."

After eight weeks in Paris the two Websters left France for England, where Noah had arranged to spend the winter working in the library of Cambridge University.

Almost immediately on arriving, he immersed himself in this work. The cold stone buildings of the University depressed him, but in the library or beside a warm fire

The arrival at Cambridge University.

in his room, he could forget this depression. Outside the dark and damp of an English winter failed to spoil his pleasure. The birds did not sing, there was no sparkling sun on winter snow as there would have been at home. Still he was happy.

The English scholars whom he met during the winter were not very cordial. To them this man from across the ocean seemed unimportant and rather bumptious. The great dictionary written by Samuel Johnson—how could anyone hope to improve it? If it were incomplete, surely the omissions were not important.

These scholars, immersed in their Greek and Latin, did not realize how the world had changed even in their own lifetimes. Science was not a popular subject with them. The story of the American Benjamin Franklin, out in the rain with a kite and a key, discovering that lightning and electricity were the same thing, did not impress them.

Americans anyhow, some of them thought, were queer creatures. Another American had come to England recently, a frowsy, backwoods man with long hair slicked down with bear's grease. This man was John James Audubon. He said he had been out in the swamps and forests along the Mississippi River for years, painting birds which no man ever saw before. Now he was in London, arranging for these pictures to be published. Hundreds and hundreds of color plates of birds in their native woodlands. But why on earth did the man refuse to cut his hair a little shorter?

At least this man, Noah Webster, made a good appearance. His neat figure, walking in the late afternoon, never offended. Black coat, well-brushed; black smallclothes fitting snugly; black silk stockings and slippers—yes, he was presentable enough. The hands folded behind his back suggested contemplation.

His eating habits, however, were said to be peculiar. More than once he had complained to his landlady about her English cooking. Those suet puddings and heavy pastries she put before him. Could he not have an apple or a handful of raisins instead? A man thought better when he ate more simply. As if a good pudding followed by a glass of port ever interfered with a man's thinking! Nevertheless, nodding over their fires after dinner, some of the English scholars had to admit that a heavy dinner did seem sometimes to lull them to sleep.

If these Americans were all alike, they would be easier to understand. The best thing probably was to go back to some good Latin author, and forget all about the Americans. Horace, at least, had been dead hundreds of years. No-one knew what he wore, or ate, or said at table. Without knowing these things it was easier to concentrate on the sterling words he had written in his books.

Meanwhile, the man in the University library went his way calmly. The day was approaching, then it was here, when his great work was finished.

"I was sitting at my table in Cambridge, England, in January, 1825," he wrote later. "When I had come to the last word I was seized with a trembling which made it difficult to proceed. However, I summoned up strength to finish the last word, and then, walking about the room a few minutes, I recovered."

The *American Dictionary of the English Language* was finished at last.

CHAPTER TWENTY-SIX

A Historic Birthday

ON THE EIGHTH of May the travelers embarked gratefully on the good ship *Hudson* for home. Five weeks at sea brought them to New York. The following day they reached New Haven.

All the family had gathered in New Haven to greet them. Emily and Julia and Harriet from their own homes, Eliza and Louisa and little Mary still under Mrs. Webster's wing. The husbands of the older girls were there, too, and a young man named Henry Jones, who intended to marry Eliza in September. Other grandchildren, besides little Mary, swelled the number still further. A full sixteen sat down to supper in honor of "Papa" and William.

Sitting at the head of his own table again, Noah Webster smiled down the long rows of happy faces. How good it was to be at home, to have around him his beloved family. He had been happy in England, but not in this warm, sweet way. If he had been a lonely scholar in a foreign country much longer he would have turned crusty.

Rebecca from her end of the table was watching him

eagerly. To her Noah was never the stern scholar with a pen like a sword, which some people thought him. Even in his most distant moments, when his work absorbed him, she saw him as her own dear husband, who needed her. At this very moment, she reflected, his beautiful hair needed trimming badly. And *what* had those foreign laundresses done to his shirts and neckcloths? The condition of his clothes, when she peeped into his baggage before supper, was truly shocking.

Little Mary, now six years old, passed up her plate for more strawberries.

"Now that Grandpa is home," she said, "I'm going to have two plates of everything."

"Only if you are a good girl!" answered Grandpa with a twinkle. "I want no bad children in my house."

"I'm not a bad girl, Grandpa," said Mary with confidence. "Only mis-*chee*-vous at times."

"What was that word you said, Mary?"

"You mean the long one? 'Mis-*chee*-vous,' Grandpa."

"Not 'mis-*chee*-vous,' Mary. '*Mis*-chi-vous.' "

Mary giggled. " 'Miss Chee vous,' " she repeated. "That way it sounds like a lady, doesn't it, Grandpa?"

" '*Mis*-chi-vous.' 'Miss *Chee* vous.' Yes, I suppose it does. But I want no such person here."

"No, of course not, Grandpa. I'll say good-by to her forever. Good-by, Miss *Chee* vous."

She waved her hand energetically.

"She's always full of fancies, Noah. Just like her

mother," said Rebecca, her eyes filling with tears.

Her husband looked at her. "All the better for that, my dear," he said quietly. "Our Mary was a ray of sunshine. Her daughter is very much like her."

A few days later Noah Webster set out on the gigantic task of getting his Dictionary published.

The first step was to find a publisher willing to undertake the work. This was not easy. The mass of material would cost a great deal to print. After six months of effort, Webster found a man in New York, Samuel Converse, who was willing to risk the money.

The next step was to check and recheck the manuscript for mistakes. This work took over a year. At last, however, the printing began—on May 8, 1827—when Webster was almost sixty-nine years old.

Proofreading required the help of three assistants. For nearly a year and a half these men toiled with Webster over the page after page of fine print that made up the *American Dictionary*. Seventy thousand words, defined in two huge volumes, were included in that first edition.

On the afternoon of October 16, 1828, Webster finished the last proof sheet. Carefully he wiped his pen, put the cork back in the ink-bottle. Then he turned to his wife, who was beside him, and suggested that they offer up a little prayer to God for having sustained him through the long task.

A few moments later his wife opened the door briskly.

"Come, dear," she said. "You know this is your birthday. Your family and friends have been waiting all day to congratulate you."

"So it is. So it is," answered her husband. "Seventy years old—threescore years and ten, as the Bible says. I had forgotten all about it."

"Well, the children and I haven't forgotten, nor the neighbors either. I told them all positively that I would have you out of your room by four o'clock."

"Rebecca, you are wonderful," answered Noah. "To work with me like this all day, and then bring on a birthday celebration without a moment's hesitation."

"Everything has been ready all day," said Rebecca. "It would be a pity, after forty years of marriage, if I couldn't provide a little celebration for you without too much bustle."

"This is the most wonderful birthday of my life," answered her husband. "And do you know, I'm quite hungry. Apparently getting the Dictionary off my hands has improved my appetite. Like Mary I'm going to have two plates of everything from now on!"

Twenty-five hundred copies of the *American Dictionary* came off the presses in November—two heavy volumes to sell for twenty dollars a set. The first two sets were put into Noah Webster's hands.

The next morning he was out early in a raw wind, harnessing his horse to the buggy.

"Where on earth are you going, dear?" asked Rebecca, when he came back into the house, blowing on his hands.

"To Westchester, New York, to present those first sets to Chief Justice John Jay."

"In this weather? Noah, you *can't*. It's forty miles to Justice Jay's home."

"But I must, Rebecca. Mr. Jay has stood by me in my work for twenty years. You know that he sent us money several times so that I could keep on with my writing. He believes in the *American Dictionary*."

"I know, dear, but surely you can send him the books. He knows that you are past seventy."

"Justice Jay is himself past eighty. This may be my last chance to do something for him. Besides, I enjoy a good drive."

"Noah, you are incorrigible. I can't do anything with you."

"You wouldn't have me an old, fretful man, would you, Becca?"

His wife looked at his fine vigorous figure and hair only slightly gray. His coloring was rosy as a boy's.

"Of course not, dear. But do wrap up warmly before you start."

The next few months brought Noah Webster the rewards for which he had been working twenty years. Praise for his great work rolled in from every side.

Teachers, who taught science or American history, wrote to say that the Dictionary was a Godsend in the classroom. Scholars, struggling to trace a word from ancient to modern times, declared that Webster's information was exactly what they needed. State legislatures voted to place a copy of the Dictionary in every school. Congress and the Supreme Court made it their official authority.

The letters which came in day after day filled Webster's heart with gratification. To a man of seventy, facing the sunset years, they offered sweet words. Noah Webster, however, did not alter his way of living on account of them. Every morning as usual he sat down early to a day's work. Before a dozen copies of the Dictionary had gone out to the subscribers he was already busy with plans for new writing.

Although he could not know it, fifteen more years of life were left him after that triumphant winter of 1828. During the first five years he made a complete new translation of the Bible and published seven new schoolbooks. One of these, a *History of the United States,* was adopted immediately in many schools. Another called *Biography,* which sketched the lives of thirty-seven famous men, became instantly popular.

His own grandchildren, who attended schools well-stocked with books, could hardly believe his tales of school life in West Hartford when he was a boy.

"What! Only three books in the whole school, Grandpa? How did you find out about American history and geography?"

"The teacher hitting the boys and girls with a stick whenever they stumbled? Oh, Grandpa!"

CHAPTER TWENTY-SEVEN

Summer Journeys

NOW THAT the Dictionary was launched successfully, the old warrior, Noah Webster, might
have expected peace and plenty. This was not
to be.

Less than a year after the great book was published
distressing news reached New Haven. Converse, the publisher, was in financial difficulties. Owing to other business ventures which failed, he could publish no more
American Dictionaries. The twenty-five hundred copies
already printed must satisfy every need, and would bring
Webster only a little more than what he had spent on
editorial assistance with the manuscript.

To his family and friends this was appalling news.

"Think of it, Noah! Twenty years of hard work, and
you make scarcely a penny out of it!" cried Rebecca. "My
poor darling!"

"Poor perhaps, Rebecca, but not an object of pity,"
answered Noah with dignity. "I have done very well all
my life on very little money. Indeed, there has scarcely
been a day since I was sixteen years old when I was not

in debt to someone. Anyone not knowing the facts would think that I was a spendthrift."

"Let anyone dare call you that!" answered Rebecca with spirit. "No man ever spent less on his own comfort. Of course," she added with a twinkle, "there have been times when we seemed to need a good many new books in spite of everything."

Her husband looked sober. "I suppose I have been selfish in that," he said. "My poor Rebecca, needing so many things for her babies, and not always knowing where the money was coming from."

"My babies had everything they needed," cried Rebecca warmly. "A good home, and a loving, devoted father."

"Not to mention a very sweet mother," added Noah gallantly. The affection between him and Rebecca had not dimmed with the years.

They were sitting during this conversation in the south front parlor of their home in New Haven, a room familiar to all their friends. Here, on either side of the fireplace, they sat during the evening, talking and rocking contentedly. Their own children and grandchildren, as well as a host of visitors, were sure to find them thus on a cold night in January or a balmy spring evening.

It was only during the summer that Noah left his domestic hearth. Every year until he was over eighty he set off gaily in July with Mary, or another of his grandchildren, on a leisurely round of visits to his married daughters. These trips he always made by horse and buggy. Long ago he had given up using the crowded stagecoaches.

Having visited one daughter, he was likely to insist that she join the party and go for a few days' visit to her nearest sister. This was pleasant enough, excepting that their father stopped so often on the way that it sometimes took days to get there. When he was riding through the country, he called on everyone he knew in the neighborhood, as well as many people he had never met before. Always he stopped at the humblest schoolhouse to see what they were teaching the children. If there was a newspaper in any town through which he was passing, he stopped to chat with the editor and read a copy of his paper.

The spelling and grammar in those country papers was sometimes far from perfect. Country editors in those days were not very particular how they spelled their words. And even though they wrote them correctly, the printer might make serious mistakes in setting the type. Often the "printer" was no more than a small boy in a smudgy apron standing on a box before a case of type. To any such boy whom he happened to meet Webster spoke long and earnestly.

"Look, my lad, you have spelled 'parlour' with a 'u'. The better way is 'parlor'. And here is a word wrong entirely."

[211]

"I guess our readers ain't so particular how we spell, mister, so long as they git to read the noos."

"Oh, but my dear Sir." The small boy almost fell off his box at the "Sir." "A newspaper sets the standard for the whole county. As you spell in your paper, people will spell in their letters and public documents. You can't afford to make mistakes."

"Maybe not, mister. Maybe not. I never thought on it much before."

"Well, think now, my lad, think now. And now tell me, why did you leave school so young, when you intended to take up printing?"

"I ain't young, mister. I was fourteen last January!"

"The time will come in this country when boys of fourteen will not give up their schooling to enter a trade. A smart lad like you could easily go through High School, and be all the better for it."

"Maybe so, mister, but my pa didn't figger it that way. He said it was high time I was earning my board and keep."

"Learning comes before earning, young man. From now on, you read everything you can lay your hands on. Everything."

"Say, mister, you set a lot of store by book-learning, don't you?"

"I surely do. All great men have been great readers and learners after they left school. You must have heard of

Benjamin Franklin. He started as a printer, you know, learning his trade just as you are."

The boy's eyes lighted.

"I've heered tell of him, mister. Our editor has a book about him. It's called *Elements of Useful Knowledge.* It tells about newspapers and such."

"You don't say so."

"A feller named Noah Webster wrote the book about Benjamin Franklin. He's wrote a dictionary, too. Our editor's ordered a copy."

"Indeed."

"Yes, sir. Our editor says this Noah Webster is quite a feller down New Haven way. He helped write the Declaration of Independence and everything."

"Not the Declaration of Independence, son, the Constitution of the United States. Noah Webster was a boy of seventeen when the Declaration of Independence was written."

"A feller of seventeen ain't a boy, mister, he's a man."

"Maybe so, my lad, maybe so. But to a man of seventy he seems more like a boy."

The boy looked at him questioningly. "Be you seventy years old, mister? You don't look that old."

"Thank you, my lad, thank you."

The boy glanced at the door a trifle uneasily.

"I'd better git back to my work now," he said. "Our editor'll skin me alive if I don't have this piece set time he gets back. He don't hold with chattering during work-ing hours."

"A very good rule, I'm sure. Good-by, Sir, good-by."

Gravely Webster shook hands, and started down the stairs to the street, where his fellow-travelers were wait-ing impatiently for him in the buggy.

"Mercy, Papa, I thought you were never coming," complained Harriet. "Who on earth were you talking to?"

"A fine lad of fourteen, who uses execrable grammar. But he will improve, he will improve. His editor has ordered a copy of the *American Dictionary.*"

"A boy of fourteen!" exclaimed Harriet. "Sometimes I think you are a boy at heart yourself, father."

"I hope so," answered Noah. "When I cease feeling that way my usefulness will be over."

"Oh, now Papa," protested Harriet. "A man your age doesn't have to feel like a shaver."

"He does to write and think for young people. And in a young country, too. Remember what your Grand-mother Webster always said. America will have a great future. You and I and Mary here are part of that great future. It is unfolding all around us."

"I know, Papa. But if we don't go a little faster, we won't get to Bridgeport by nightfall."

" 'Tis no matter, no matter, dear," said her father good-humoredly. "If we don't arrive today, we will tomorrow. This driving all day in the fresh air makes me feel like a boy again. I only wish your mother had come with us."

"She finds it hard sitting in the buggy so much. If I didn't love the open air, I'd say the same myself."

"Of course, dear. I'm a selfish old man to make you."

And slapping the reins vigorously on the mare's back, Noah put her into a brisk trot.

CHAPTER TWENTY-EIGHT

The End of a Great Spirit

T HE YEARS passed rapidly enough, with Webster having only one grievance. The first edition of his *Dictionary* was exhausted: no more copies were available. Like a worm in an apple, this fact gnawed at his happiness.

In the year 1838 he celebrated his eightieth birthday. Family and friends gathering to congratulate him were astonished to find him shut up in his room.

"But this is his *birthday*," they protested to Rebecca. "Surely we may see him."

"Yes indeed, at four o'clock," answered Rebecca. "Some proofs came yesterday. He is correcting them now."

When he came out of his study, Noah was buoyant with pleasure.

"A very happy day this," he said. "Thank you all for coming."

"I don't see how you do it, Mr. Webster," said one of his visitors, marveling at his thick hair and ruddy complexion. "Tell us the secret of your long, healthy life."

"Certainly," answered Noah heartily. "I have always

retired early and risen with the lark . . . I have combined bodily exercise with mental labor."

To this he might well have added that, in spite of many hardships, he had always done work which he heartily enjoyed. Words and their meanings were meat and drink to him; he would never stop working with them until he died. If only he could find someone to bring out a second edition of his Dictionary, now that the first one was exhausted and the original publisher in bankruptcy.

Today, however, on his eightieth birthday a happy solution had come to him. He would mortgage his home in New Haven to pay for a new edition. The proofreading he could do himself. Although he had worn glasses for a number of years, his keen eyes were equal to any emergency. No wonder he was happy that October afternoon with his family around him.

The family, of course, threw up their hands in horror, when he revealed his bold plan to them.

"Father, you *can't* at your age," they wailed. "You are risking the roof over your head."

"I shan't need a roof over my head much longer," answered Noah calmly. "And this country does need more dictionaries. Surely the merest child can see that."

The more they tried to argue with him, the more stubbornly he insisted that his plan was sensible in every particular. Rebecca, who had learned long ago that she was married to a stubborn Connecticut Yankee, did not argue with him at all. And so it was that before his next birthday a new printing of the *American Dictionary* was under way. A year later the famous edition of 1840 was ready for distribution.

Noah Webster did not live to see bigger and better editions of his dictionary published, but these have appeared regularly at intervals during the last hundred years. A popular, one-volume edition, selling for six dollars, came in 1847. The famous *Unabridged* edition was published in 1864, with 175,000 words to the original 70,000. The *New International* edition of 1909, revised in 1934, contained 600,000 words.

How Noah Webster would have reveled in the growth of his great work. Like a snowball rolling down the years, his Dictionary has gathered force and momentum. The new words which came into the language after the year 1840 would have left even Noah Webster gasping—words like telephone, telegraph, automobile, steam-engine, sewing-machine, radio, refrigerator, air-plane, bomb-sight and blitz. Other dictionaries have come and gone, but since 1864 no-one has seriously questioned the fact that Webster's Dictionary, with its subsequent editing, is the finest book of its kind in the English language.

Meanwhile, what of Noah Webster himself after the great edition of 1840 was published? He did not lose his home by his venture. Every evening, when his day's work was finished, he and Rebecca sat rocking and reading in their friendly parlor. Friends came and went. Some of the children were always visiting.

Until Sunday, the twenty-first of May, 1843, there was no change in this comfortable routine. On that day, however, he remarked to a friend that his "literary labors were almost finished. From now on," he continued quietly, "I intend to spend more time in my garden."

The garden never saw him again. The following day he caught cold, and by Friday he was very ill with a fever. Two days later he died peacefully during the evening. If he had lived another five months, he would have reached his eighty-fifth birthday.

About the Author

ISABEL PROUDFIT is well known in the book field. She has written biographies of Hans Christian Andersen, Robert Louis Stevenson, Mark Twain, Noah Webster, James Fenimore Cooper. She has also written charming stories for young children, some of which have appeared in book form, others in children's magazines. Before turning to juvenile writing, Mrs. Proudfit was a reporter covering important assignments for newspapers in New York City and London. Although her childhood was spent in Illinois, she lived for many years on a farm in Connecticut and now makes her home in New York City.